D0430635

Celebrate
Yourself!

# Celebrate Yourself!

## And Other Inspirational Essays

### ERIC BUTTERWORTH

UNITY® Books

**Unity Village, Missouri**

Fourth printing 1997

Copyright © 1984 by Unity School of Christianity. All rights reserved. No part of this book may be used or reproduced in any manner whatsoever without written permission from Unity School of Christianity except in the case of brief quotations embodied in critical articles and reviews or in the newsletters and lesson plans of licensed Unity teachers and ministers. For information, address Unity Books, Publishers, Unity School of Christianity, 1901 NW Blue Parkway, Unity Village, MO 64065-0001.

To receive a catalog of all Unity publications (books, cassettes, compact discs, and magazines) or to place an order, call the Customer Service Department: (816) 969-2069 or 1-800-669-0282.

Cover design by Carla Jones
Illustration by Joe Breeden

Library of Congress Catalog Card Number: 84-051318
ISBN 0-87159-207-X
Canada BN 13252 9033 RT

Unity Books feels a sacred trust to be a healing presence in the world. By printing with biodegradable soybean ink on recycled paper, we believe we are doing our part to be wise stewards of our Earth's resources.

# Contents

# Contents

*Introduction*

The study of Truth is much more than a mere gathering of information. It is a process of *out*formation. A teacher or a book such as this one should be more than a fuel pipe for infusing ideas. It should become a spark plug to ignite your hidden potential where "Truth abides in fullness."

The goal of these pages is not simply to expose you to some Truth words, but rather to redirect the focus of your mind toward Truth. It has been wisely said that when you have forgotten all that you have read or heard, what remains in your consciousness is what you have learned.

This book is composed of intentionally succinct essays covering a broad spectrum of human needs. Each piece is a trenchant flow of crisp and pithy ideas to challenge your mind. Each is a digest of an extensive dissertation, which you will reassemble in your mind as you read creatively.

What matters is not what is in the book, but what unfolds in your mind as you read the book. The "gospel" according to Eric Butterworth is only of passing significance. As far as your unfoldment is concerned, all that matters is the gospel according to you. The world tells us many things, some that are hearsay and some that are fact. We may read the Scriptures and affirm many Truths, but what really counts is what we are saying to ourselves.

You cannot get away from yourself, no matter where you go. You are always environed by yourself, horizoned by your mentality, encircled by your ideals, and constantly influenced by what you are saying to yourself. What you think within yourself and what you say to yourself is what determines the life you experience, the health you express, and the prosperity you demonstrate.

In many cases the study of Truth is a study of words, intellectual concepts, or interpretations of the Scriptures. There is a tendency to view the words as objects, to deal with them with little short of worship. Words of Truth should be seen as windows through which we view things and find the Truth in ourselves. The ultimate Truth for you, at this point in time, is the gospel according to you.

For the most effective use of this book, don't read more than one essay at a sitting. Spend at least fifteen minutes thinking on its ideas. Read and reread, underlining and making notations in the margins. It is your book. Use it! If time permits (and the sincere student will always *make* time), lay the book aside in an experience of silence or meditation. The important thing for your growth is not what the book brings *to* you, but what awakens within you and flows forth *through* you. This will become your gospel.

# Celebrate Yourself!

It has been said: *When the ties that bind the mind are broken and a person is introduced to his real self that has no limitations, the bells of heaven ring for joy.* This is what Jesus had in mind when He said: "*... it is your Father's good pleasure to give you the kingdom.*" (Luke 12:32). As the universe rushes and streams into you from all sides, it is a veritable cosmic celebration of ecstasy. It could be said, and should be, that you are the universe celebrating itself as you.

One wonders why many of us who seem to be intelligent persons let thoughts that corrode our minds blind us to the sheer thrill of living. The truly intelligent person is one who can grasp the fact that it is a curious experience to be alive, so curious in fact that it is

1

madness not to sacrifice everything to get the full taste of being alive. The question each of us needs to ask himself is, "What am I willing to sacrifice to get the full taste of life?"

Shortly before he died, Thomas Edison was asked to define electricity. He said, impatiently: *No one really knows what it is, only what it does. But it exists. Use it!* Not Jesus nor all the mystics of all time have been able to define the infinite power within us. But they have all implied in their teachings: It exists. Use it!

Charles Fillmore said that life for each of us should be a "journey in jubilance." This implies a willingness to let life be a constant experience of celebration. Thomas Carlyle had this in mind when he said: *Every day that is born into the world comes like a burst of music and rings the whole day through, and you make of it a dance, a dirge, or a life-march, as you will.*

This does not imply the license to live indulgently and superficially. Many celebrations are mere excuses for overindulgence, with noisemakers, loud salutations, and so on, revealing that it is a cover for personal meaninglessness and the desire to escape. It is not unlike involvement in a religious celebration, which is often an escape in a more pious setting. The problem is, though we may celebrate the rite, we may not celebrate ourselves. It could be said that the mere worship of God is hypocritical unless it leads to a deeper sense of personal "worth-ship."

The word *celebrate* means *to honor.* It does not imply dealing with something that is done, as from the outside. Rather it is giving a very special blessing *to* something. In the true spirit of celebration you are not just a loud-laughing spectator. You are an involved participant. You become a conscious channel for the cosmic flow.

In a celebration consciousness you can look around you and bless your family, friends, and co-workers as fellow travelers along the journey of life. As you make your way to or from work, if you can bless the sunshine or the clouds, the trees and grass and flowers, the friendly people in the park, you are truly rich. Without this sense of celebration, you are poor no matter what your net worth may be.

Edmond Rostand gives a creative meaning to the word celebration in his classic work, *The Chanticleer.* He tells the poignant story of a rooster who crowed lustily every morning at sunrise, but who actually thought it was his crowing that caused the sun to rise. It gave him a sense of significance. His life mattered. One morning he overslept. He rushed to his post atop the henhouse, only to find that the sun had already risen without him. His dreamworld collapsed as he realized his self-delusion. But then, to his mind came a great thought, equal to the wisdom of a sage: *It may be that my crowing does not cause the sun to rise, but I can still awake to celebrate its rising.*

A person was pouring out her heart in concern over changing circumstances in her life. She said, "But now I have nothing to live for, nothing to look forward to." How common is this attitude of fear! It is the fear of being in a position of having nothing to celebrate. But you can, like Chanticleer, get into a celebration consciousness—not just dealing with something "out there," but celebrating *from* something within.

Walt Whitman has been mercilessly abused for his beautiful declaration, "I celebrate myself!" Few persons have understood that this was a conscious commitment to let the universe celebrate itself through him. It is the celebration consciousness, not looking forward to things, but looking forward from an inward flame of life.

Take time to be still and listen to the beat of your heart and feel the throb of your pulse. The universe is celebrating itself in you as an instrument of life. It is singing itself into your soul, saying, "You are alive, you are whole, and you are being healed and renewed in a constant rhapsody of life." Celebrate yourself. Say yes to life, to health, to renewal. Sing your song of wholeness.

This is what work is, or should be—a celebration of yourself. Kahlil Gibran says if you cannot work with love but only with distaste, then you should quit your job and go to the temple and beg alms from those who work with joy. Get a new insight into the creative flow involved in labor. Celebrate yourself in your work.

This is what love is, a great celebration. It is the great heart of the universe streaming into and through you, and willingness to let it shine. When you really understand what love is, you find that by loving you ennoble yourself, you are in tune with the cosmic flow. Get a sense right now of the infinite heart of God flowing forth through you and out to embrace all the persons in your world. Celebrate yourself through love.

This is what joy is, a celebration of life. But let's be sure we understand the process of happiness, or else we might sometimes say, "I am unhappy because there is nothing in my life to celebrate." The thought is predominant with most persons that happiness comes from relationships and experiences. The fact is, the happy life is one that is in tune with the inner flow. When you are inwardly centered, you are happy. And your happiness is not the effect of things or conditions, but more likely the cause of them. The poet sings: *All things respond to the call of rejoicing, all things gather where life is a song.*

Begin your day, every day, in a celebration consciousness. Within you is the unborn possibility of limitless life, and yours is the joyous privilege of giving birth to it. Let the child of your great potential be born. Happy birthday! The universe is celebrating you. Celebrate yourself!

# The Mystery of God in Man

Within every person is the unborn possibility of limitless growth, and ours is the privilege of giving birth to it. Paul obviously had this in mind when he referred to: ... *the mystery hidden for ages and generations ... which is Christ in you, the hope of glory* (Col. 1:26, 27).

Studies of God have abounded in all the religions of the world, most of which have dealt with an intellectual construction of a Being "out there." And we have been subtly conditioned by artists' visualizations such as Michelangelo's classic frescoes on the ceiling of the Sistine Chapel in Vatican City. A massive figure of a man, representing the Almighty, reaches down to touch man. It is a beautiful work of art, but not the best ex-

7

ample of man's attempt to define the indefinable.

Through the ages of man's quest for Truth and reality, there has appeared, here and there, a lone figure who caught the idea of the mystery of God in man. Ikhnaton, King of Egypt from 1379-1362 B.C., was a forerunner of the ideal. His is probably the first awareness of "God is one and man is one in that one." Among the Greek philosophers, Plotinus stands out as a forerunner of the new insight of Truth. He caught the idea of a cosmic force that is both imminent and transcendent in life. *Each being contains in itself the whole intelligible world. Therefore all is everywhere. Each is all, and all is each.* He saw man at the very center of the universe which rushes and streams and pours into him from all sides while he stands quietly.

But for the most part, this idea of God in man has been a well-kept secret in the field of religion, and a rejected theory in science. This could well be the most colossal blunder ever made by man, for while man has searched the heavens and the Earth, the great secret of existence lies within himself. It is only through realizing this mystery of God in man that we can understand one like Jesus, with all His spiritual power, as a demonstration of that which is fundamental in all life.

Dwell for a while on the idea of the universe as the allness that we call God, realizing that everything within it, from the vast galaxies to the subatomic particles, is created in and of the universe. You may wonder about the vastness of the universe and peer at it through a telescope. However, you are not on the outside looking in. You are on the inside looking out. You are the universe at the point where you are.

Attributed to Saint Augustine is this profound thought: *God is a circle whose center is everywhere and whose circumference is nowhere.* If the center is everywhere, it is where you are. You are the center of the universe, the center of God. This is not a point to be made egotistically, but transcendentally. There is that of you which is centered in God, and which is a point of God-activity flowing forth into expression as you. And, the circumference is limitless. There is no limit to God, or to man in God consciousness.

God is not in you like a raisin is in a roll, but like the ocean is in a wave. The wave is nothing more nor less than the ocean formed into the shape of a wave. And you are nothing

9

more nor less than God expressing as you.
Thus divine sonship is not a projection of the
Divine into the human. God cannot project
Himself outside Himself; He can only express
Himself within Himself. Man is not an indi-
vidual in God, for that would presuppose iso-
lation and separation. Man is an individual-
ization of God.

This is fundamental for all persons. Thus,
any kind of phenomena displayed by uncommon men and women are but the erratic manifestation of a higher state of consciousness
that will be the natural possession of the man
of the future. As Jesus said: "... *he who
believes in me will also do the works that I do;
and greater works than these will he do* ..."
(John 14:12). God in each of us is the allness
of which we are an eachness, and the constant
need in our lives is to unfold more of our allness in a process of conscious evolution. It is
not trying to get into God or to get God into
us. It is to, *"Be still, and know that I am
God"* (Psalms 46:10).

We all have a long way to go, but Jesus
demonstrated a goal that is believable and
achievable, and He pointed to that in us
which is perfectible. Wherever we are along
the way, no matter what the problems or

challenges, there is always more in us, the Christ in us as our *hope of glory,* which means our potential for healing, overcoming, prospering, and succeeding. And there is no limit!

## *The Power of "Amen"*

The word *amen* is one of the most vital and powerful words in our language, and yet it has been lost to us for all practical purposes by its routine liturgical use. In the immortal *Macbeth,* Shakespeare has one of his players say: *"I had most need of a blessing, and Amen stuck in my throat."* One of the reasons we have such meager results from our prayers is that, figuratively, *amen* sticks in our throats.

In the original language of the Bible the word *amen* meant "verily, it is established, this is the truth." For instance, in the first chapter of Genesis where we read: *And God said ... And it was so,* the "it was so" was originally "Amen." The Gospels originally had Jesus saying: *"Amen, Amen, I say unto thee.*" However, English translations have changed this to: "*Verily, verily, I say unto you.*"

In Isaiah 65:16 we read: "*. . . he who blesses himself in the land shall bless himself by the God of truth . . . .*" There is a marginal note that indicates that "*the God of truth*" was originally "*amen.*" Thus, we can see that this word has a mystical and powerful meaning.

The ancient Egyptians realized the power of amen and incorporated it into the name of their greatest leaders. There were Pharaoh Amenhotep, Tutankamen, and Amen-Ra. Amen to the Egyptians meant master or ruler. Whatever you unite your amen to, you declare to be a fixed and final Truth, and it promptly assumes mastery over your life.

When we see the true meaning of amen, we see the error in our ways of praying in the traditional manner: "O God, I am sick and troubled; help me. Amen." It is a typical way of beseeching, but we are actually saying amen to that which we do not want. We are saying to sickness and trouble, "This is the Truth. I believe it. I accept it." We should never formulate and voice a prayer that we are not willing to declare to be a fixed Truth, nor should we add amen to such a prayer.

13

To what are you saying amen? When you hear a medical report that presents a dark and hopeless picture, do you accept it with resignation? When you are told that you are too old to find a job, do you give in to the idea and prepare for the inevitable? If so, you are saying amen to these things, thus giving strength to them in your life.

Paul says: *For all the promises of God find their Yes in him. That is why we utter the Amen through him, to the glory of God* (II Cor. 1:20). This has several important meanings. We must reject the negative, limited, and weak thoughts expressed about us. We must hold to and affirm the positive and constructive.

But we must do more than speak words of Truth. We must accept the reality they affirm. One may declare a Truth, such as: *I am strong and whole now.* Then he may later say, "Well, I used the affirmation; I sure hope it works." He has forgotten to say amen to the Truth. His prayer concludes with a question mark instead of a period. Speak the word of Truth, and then say amen to it with finality, meaning, and the belief that it is done, so be it.

I am not suggesting a broader use of the

word *amen* or the traditional prayer that usually accompanies it. But I do say, be careful that you say amen, literally and figuratively, only to those things that are good and true, to what you want to see manifest in your life. May you be blessed with all that is good. Amen.

## *How to Turn Your Life Around*

If you are not happy with the things that
are repeatedly happening in your life, or with
the direction in which you seem to be moving,
you can turn it around. But first you must
understand that it is *your* life, that you live in
a world of your own thoughts, and that you
can change your life by altering your
thoughts whenever you really want to do so.
This is not to say it is easy, but it is possible.

Life is consciousness. You stand where you
do today, wherever that is, because of your
consciousness. And there is only one way you
can come to stand anywhere else—by changing your consciousness. If you wish to go up
higher, you can do so, and there is no limit to
the heights to which you can climb. But you
must "repent," which means to be ... *trans-*

*formed by the renewal of your mind . . .* (Rom. 12:2).

Jesus said: *"In the world you have tribulation; but be of good cheer, I have overcome the world"* (John 16:33). There is a level of life where states of consciousness give rise to limited conditions, and where a cycle of causation flows in a kind of negative momentum. *"I have overcome the world"* means getting into a higher level of consciousness, experiencing freedom from the limited cycle of causation.

If you are unemployed, you may feel "out of it." To turn this experience around, you must get out of the "out of it" consciousness, and get into the "with it" and "in it" feeling. You may pray for work and get another job, but unless you have reversed the patterns of consciousness that led to unemployment, you have only temporarily solved the problem. One person was excitedly testifying to the value of Truth in his life, "I have demonstrated three jobs in the past year!" This is a hard way to go about it!

*"I have overcome the world."* Get into a higher level of consciousness. Stop thinking of work as something to demonstrate "out there." Get the feeling that it is a part of your

17

nature, that work comes *through* you and not *to* you. If you are unemployed, get the feeling that you are ready for work. Think movement, activity, work, service.

A man on welfare for ten years, discovering that the experience crippled him in terms of his self-worth, volunteered in a special program of community service. It could be the means of turning his life around, for in the process of work, even without pay, he will open up within him the flow of creativity. Countless human lives could well be salvaged if his example were followed.

If you are not satisfied with the direction your life has taken, or with the experiences that continually manifest, you can change by getting into the kind of attitudes and feelings that you assume you would have if you were now experiencing the desired conditions. You may object, "But I feel tired and defeated; how can I help that?" Feelings are not beyond the control of the will. You are not your feelings. You *have* feelings, and the you that has feelings can control them and reverse them.

It is never too late to turn your life around, to break the patterns of negativity that keep manifesting themselves as age and deterioration, as inharmony and loneliness, as illness and physical discomfort, and as financial insecurity and lack. You will have to "repent" and follow the higher way of living and thinking. Wake up from your self-limiting thought to self-releasing vertical thought, and you will experience the ceaseless flow of your own good.

## The Divine Equation

The exploration of space has been one of the most exciting developments of this century. Whatever else we ultimately find the universe to be, it is whole. We may not see or understand the whole, even the whole of the point where we exist, but it is whole, and in that we may feel secure. Nothing can be taken out of the universe; thus, nothing is ever irrelevant. This means that you are important; you are whole.

The great message of Jesus was wholeness, oneness. He said: *"I and the Father are one"* (John 10:30). His real meaning has been obscured because people have thought of Jesus as "very God," His relationship with God being unique. Actually, Jesus was outlining the divine equation: I + the Father = one. Jesus was articulating the principle of "universal unity." He was saying, "You live in the universe, and you are a part within the whole. However, the whole is also within you, and there can never be a separation." According to a Unity principle, the whole of Spirit is present in its entirety at every point in space at the same time. This means that God in man *is* the Holy Spirit, or the whole of Spirit. The whole of mind, the whole of love, the whole of substance is in me and is in focus as me at every moment in time and at every point in space.

The goal of every Truth seeker is to grow spiritually. But you do not have to become spiritual; you are spiritual—all that you can ever be. The quest is to become a whole person. But you are already a whole person. The need is to become aware of your underlying reality. That is what healing is.

This is a concept that Jan Christiaan Smuts calls "holism." He says: *Wholes are basic to the character of the universe, and holism, as the operative factor in the evolution of wholes, is the ultimate principle of the universe.* In other words, the seed can become the tree because the tree is in the seed. And you can become what you desire to be be-

cause the Christ, your infinite potential, is
within you. No matter in what stage the plant
may be between the seed and the tree, the
potential whole is always in the part. No matter what your experience may be, there is
always an allness within the illness, an all-
sufficiency within any insufficiency, and so
on. Whatever is, is whole, whether or not you
can see or experience that wholeness.

It is not always easy to see wholeness in
the face of limitations. Seeing may be the key
to understanding and applying the Truth. If
you really see a thing, you need nothing more.
We tend to see in part; thus with a frag-
mented perspective, we judge by appearances. The need is to see things as one, to see
together. Actually, the word *consciousness*
literally means "to see together."

Jesus urges us to judge righteous judgment, which means to see the whole in the
part. It is to see one-to-one. "One" is the
whole of you, and the other "one" is the
whole of the other person. This one-to-one
perception is effective in dealing with financial difficulties. It is to see from your oneness
with the divine flow within you, and to relate
to the job, the business venture, or the
general economy in that same sense of one-

ness. When you are dealing with things on the one-to-one basis, you will insist that things are one-derful, which is an interesting and helpful variation on the word. People may ask, "How are things?" You can reply, "Oh, things are one-derful." They may not realize it, but you are voicing something more than optimism.

Of course, you will be positive and optimistic, too. For how can you "daub with sables and gloom" when you know that the whole is present in every part? How can you doubt or fear or worry when you realize that everything and everyone is full of oneness and thus, one-derful?

When you become a whole person, in terms of the positive outlook on life, you project the kind of vibration that has a healing, harmonizing, and prospering influence. You can bet that the happy person will have the least illness, the confident person will have the greatest chance for success, and the positive thinker will seem to have all the good luck.

Of course, this takes some doing. We often require unruly children in Sunday school to stand before their peers and say, "I am a child of God and I act like one." When we find ourselves disturbed or down, or coming apart at the seams, we need to say to ourselves, "You are a whole person, and it is high time you started acting like one!" There may be challenges and challenging personalities, but you can cope because the whole of Spirit is always within you. You are one-derful. You are whole.

# The Law of Attraction

"... to him who has will more be given, and he will have abundance; but from him who has not, even what he has will be taken away" (Matt. 13:12). This statement of Jesus is difficult for many persons to understand. It is really quite simple: a magnet attracts and holds iron filings. If it were unmagnetized, the same steel would attract nothing. If you were to heap some filings on the steel, they would fall off at the first jostling.

We can never understand Truth or life until we give up, once and for all, the idea of favoritism in the universe, and until we stop praying to be forgiven before we have changed our own attitudes. God plays no favorites. If you have your finger in a socket and are being shocked, you can pray all you want, but nothing will happen until you remove your finger.

One may say, "I was driving along, minding my own business, and a car careened around a corner and ran into the side of my car. What did I do to deserve that?" An insurance company report says that ninety percent of all accidents result from unconscious volition. This means that some people are accident-prone. Things always seem to happen to them, not by the caprice of God or by bad luck, but by the law of attraction. Bad luck is simply a bad mental habit. You make the difference!

There are no experiences unrelated to the consciousness of all who may be involved. Every person is a living magnet, drawing to himself things, people, and circumstances in accord with his thoughts. The man may say, "But I was not thinking about accidents!" However, in the subconscious mind there must have been patterns of belief in accidents as a possibility, resistance of careless drivers, or fear of being on the road, and others. You may recall a time when drivers of all the cars were "rubbernecking" (gawking) at a highway mishap—accepting the idea into their consciousness, laying up pools of limitation in their minds. A good policy for such an experience: if there is something you can do in an emergency, by all means get out and do it. If not, bless the people involved, say no to the negatives involved, shake the dust off your feet, and move on.

If you are having a problem, don't shift into the attitude that a "twist of fate has ruined my life." This is a cop-out. The experience has happened, and to you, not to someone else. At this time, you may not understand it, but something in you has attracted it. Don't grovel in the "why," for this may be a subtle attempt to vindicate yourself and to implicate someone or something else. Accept the obvious fact that it has happened, and know that there is that in you that is equal to it. And most importantly, determine that you will grow through it and thus rise to a state of mind where such a thing cannot happen again.

Jesus said: "... *lay up for yourselves treasures in heaven* ..." (Matt. 6:20). This implies building positive realizations into your consciousness. It is like incarnating magnetism into the steel. The man with the car should be grateful that the experience has revealed where he is. Now he can alter his thoughts and regularly prepare himself for driving by affirming: *The Spirit of the Lord goes before me to make safe, joyous, and successful my way.*

When someone leaves on a trip or starts a new job, it is common to be expected to say, "Good luck!" This is a subtle negative introducing the possibility of danger, with the hope that his number does not come up. Never wish anyone good luck or pray for good luck for yourself. Rather, say: "I bless you with success," or simply, "Success!" And for yourself: *God's law of adjustment regulates all the affairs of my life, and all things are in divine order.*

Negative vibrations are everywhere: on the street, on television, in private conversations, and so on. Be alert to your feelings, and settle with things quickly by remembering the Truth. You don't have to make a nuisance of yourself by criticizing negative people. Two negatives do not make a positive. But you can deal with negatives using a kind of neutrality and not being negative yourself. Remember, it is your mind and you cannot afford to have pockets of poison in it.

Why not revive the old idea of blessing? Neutralize negatives; bless them (which is to know the Truth about them) and project a flow of love and light that dissolves them as far as you are concerned. When you hear, read, or see something negative, instead of saying, "Oh my, isn't that simply awful?" bless it, and know the Truth about it.

Begin every day not hoping for luck, but affirming: *This is a wonderful day, and I am a magnet for only the good in it.*

# The Universe and You

*The whole theory of the universe is directed unerringly to one single individual—namely to You.* Walt Whitman is saying that the universe has meaning only as it helps you to define yourself, and your life has no meaning except as an integral part of the universe.

As far as you are concerned the universe exists as an extension of you, even as your whole body exists as an extension of your little finger. When you move your little finger, your entire body is actually involved, and similarly, the entire universe is involved in what you think, feel, and do.

If you look into the world that the microscope cannot encompass and into the world of space that the telescope cannot reach, you will note that everywhere there is pattern and plan, order and rhythm, energy and intelligence. You will see subatomic particles acting like planets in orbit around the sun. And the realization will dawn in your consciousness that the reality of the universe is not in what you see, but in what you cannot see; not in the planets or the particles, but in the forces that hold them in their courses.

As you see a movement of energy everywhere, it becomes obvious that in the air, in the water, on and in the earth everything seems alive and moving. But the important thing is that you are alive, you think, you feel, you experience. All that surrounds you in the vast cosmos, from the infinitely great to the miniscule, has meaning because you have meaning.

The universe is abundant and unlimited in every respect. If it were limited it would have long since depleted itself. There is always enough of everything to go around. You may say, "For a person of my years, I do pretty well. After all, life takes its toll." Nonsense! There is no premium to living. There is enough life for all persons and for all time. You may say, "After what he did to me, I can never love him again." Why not? Has love suddenly disappeared? Love, like life, does not come and go. And it can know no depletion. Love is. There is always enough love to go around.

The continued use of a principle never exhausts the principle. Thus, as the expression of the universal God-principle, you can never exhaust the potential of life or wisdom or love or substance. Why, then, should one go through life impoverished in a universe that is opulent? Life is not something to be endured. It is to be lived abundantly. Every person should be limitless, living in a heaven of accomplishment. Yet many persons live in fear and war and poverty and sickness, and that which they fear comes upon them.

One of the problems of our time is that in living and moving in vast crowds we tend to become depersonalized. We lose perspective of ourselves and our relationship to one another and to life and the universe. We tend to live at the circumference of our being and to become totally other-directed. Happy conditions make for our happiness, and inharmonious conditions make for confusion and inner conflict. We lose sight of our uniqueness as integral parts of the universe.

The need is to be still and listen, and let God sing His song through you. Look away from the lonely nobody in the crowd that you may have been seeing yourself as being, and look to the larger concept where the whole universe has meaning because of you. Let these words indicate a total giving way to the flow within you: *No matter how unimportant what I do may seem to me, it could not be done in quite the same way without me to do it. I am important, for I am God's melody of life singing itself into the continuum. The music of the spheres would not be complete without my voice. God needs me, not as I think I should be but feel somehow that I am not, but as I am.*

Listen to the voice of silence within. It is saying to you, "You are a unique and wonderful individual. You are important. You are not just a statistic, but a vital part of the universe. Truly you live in its center. You are its center. You are God's living enterprise. God has something wonderful to say through you which He can only say as you. The cosmos can never be quite complete without you."

*Thou hast given him dominion over the works of thy hands; thou hast put all things under his feet . . .* (Psalms 8:6).

33

## The Secret of Thought Control

It is often written, "You are what you think." It is not really accurate, for you are *thinking* what you think. The secret that is rarely discovered is the realization that you are not a mind. You *have* a mind, and the you that has a mind can control the thoughts that pass through the mind. This is not to say that this control is easy, but it can be done.

Thought is a creative process, or should be. You can become a creative thinker instead of a reactive thinker. Just remember, it is *your* mind and you can think what you want to think. You must stop letting your grandfather do your thinking for you—or your church, or the media, or the people who irritate you. Whether you know it or not, the choice is yours, whether you react, and thus permit people or conditions to determine how you think, or whether you think the kind of thoughts that you really want to see manifest in your life.

At least once a day in meditation, "dis-identify" from your mind so that you can become established at the center of your being as the master of your life. Then, carefully established at the center of your spiritual gravity, you are ready to deal creatively with anything that may happen around you and to you.

All that you read in the papers or hear on the news, all that may come to you in the demands of your employers or the temperament of your co-workers will become what you accept it as being. You always have a choice! You may say, "Of course I am bitter and upset, look what I have had to face!" But that is a cop-out. It is your mind. Never forget it!

When you are established at the center of your being, you can control what goes on in your mind. You can read the news and talk to people, but you will not worship at the altar of "they say." Cultivate your own convictions, develop your own opinions—not to make you opinionated, but to enable you to really assume control over your life by the discipline of your mind. Do not settle comfortably into the "custom-made" convictions of a church or a political party.

A vital part of controlling thought is the evaluation that you place on what you see. As far as you are concerned things will always be to you what you see them as being. So look for the good, see all things in the light of Truth. Don't try to set things right; just be sure that you see them rightly. When you see things in the right perspective, you establish your mastery, for you allow them entrance into your consciousness on your terms.

There is a distinction between thinking the thoughts you want to think about things and following the superficial practice of positive thinking. For the latter can be a kind of custom-made thinking where someone gives you the platitudes to parrot, and you go through the whole day memorizing and mouthing metaphysical clichés. Most persons will not detect your superficial approach to life, but divine law does. As Emerson says: *What you are stands over you the while, and thunders so that I cannot hear what you say to the contrary.*

The controlled mind is not a mind that never has a negative thought. Even Jesus had negative thoughts. In His wilderness experience Satan tried three times to lure Him to use His powers for selfish ends. This was no demon actually having being "out there." It was the influence of Jesus' own human consciousness. Jesus, however, quickly disidentified from the evil force, saying, *"Get thee hence!"* As someone put it: *You may not be able to stop the birds from flying over your head, but you can keep them from building a nest in your hair.* You may not always keep negative thoughts out of your mind, but you can determine that you are in control.

Some persons are influenced into negative thinking because of their sympathetic approach toward life. It is as if they feel that when people have tribulations, it is their duty to "tribulate." They read the daily paper with a heavy heart; so much trouble in the world, so much pain and injustice! The hardened pessimist will insist that things are as they are and that one is blind to refuse to see the "terrible things that are going on." He may say, "I just call a spade a spade. I am not going to say I don't have problems when the world is beating on me."

It is interesting and revealing that those who have taken the hardest blows have been the greatest people. Their handicaps have only spurred them on to greater efforts, which is to say that they did not succeed in spite of their limitations, but because of them. William Ernest Henley was in a hospital, racked with the pain of a "hopelessly incurable" ailment. It was here that he wrote the classic lines: *I am the master of my fate: I am the captain of my soul.* The pessimist may feel justified in feelings of discouragement and injustice. But Henley disidentified himself from the experience of the body and from the negative tendencies of the mind.

Begin every day at the beginning, which means return to the foundation principle: God is One, and you are One with Him. Center yourself at your spiritual center of gravity. You are not your mind; you have a mind, and you have the power to control its function. You can change your life by altering your thoughts. And you can control your thoughts and take complete charge of your life.

## The Law of Vibration

Vibration is everywhere, at the root of all things. Even the "simple" act of voice communication is really not so simple. Thought vibrations in one person lead to vibrating vocal cords sending forth sound waves that vibrate another's ear drums; then the vibrations are decoded into some kind of awareness leading to thought vibrations in the other person.

In New York City is Avery Fisher Hall, one of the greatest music halls in the world. This music hall, devoted to symphonic music, is itself a symphony. The walls are made of materials composed of atoms in vibration. The design of the building is a "tone poem." Johann Goethe, a German poet and dramatist, referred to architecture as "frozen music," a beautiful description.

If you look at your body in a mirror, you actually see an illusion. The ratio between the mass of subatomic particles and the vast spaces between is like chicken wire of the thinnest steel wire and the gaping open areas within it. Squeeze out all the space of your body and you will have the bulk of a speck of dust. And yet, when those particles are singing their song of life, you have a body that breathes and walks and talks and dances. You are vibration.

One of the benefits of attending a religious service in a church or cathedral (or music hall) over simply reading spiritual things out of a book is that a response is felt in the cells and functions of the body as a healing influence. When the vibration of the body temple is synchronized with powerfully spoken words of Truth and the fine vibrations of the sanctuary and the collective expectations of the congregation, there is a transforming influence. To those who can get synchronized with the positive vibrations, every service is a healing service.

Of course, you may not always be in situations where the vibrations are good. You may be unhappy about the bad vibrations at work, in your neighborhood, even in your own home. Jesus said: *"Agree with thine adversary quickly ... "* (Matt. 5:25 A.V.). Don't be misled; He is talking about *your* adverse reaction, the bad vibration of *your* resistance. To "agree," as He uses the term, means to get in tune with God, to become synchronized with the divine flow. When you are poised in yourself, you are in a position to project this positive vibration to the world.

Ask yourself, "Am I part of the solution to the problems around me, or am I part of the problem?" If you react with anger or bitterness or fear, you are projecting negative vibrations, and thus you are part of the problem. Unless you want to perpetuate conditions around you, you must change your thoughts about them.

Jesus said to let your light shine. One with positive vibrations of light emanating from him can walk into a room and his presence is immediately felt as a harmonizing influence. On the other hand, Al Capp caricatures the one who walks in darkness: Joe Btfsk walks with a dark cloud over him, spreading entropy wherever he goes. Hens do not lay, cars will not start, people cannot get along.

We need to work constantly to heighten

our consciousness, to build positive vibrations within. We do this most effectively through the power of the spoken word. Charles Fillmore says: *Words are the most powerful agents of the mind. Every time we speak we cause the atoms of the body to tremble and change their places.*

When you speak you send forth vibrations that the Bible says have the power of life and death. Isaiah says: *Woe to those who decree iniquitous decrees . . .* (Isa. 10:1). Many of our woes might very well be traced back to such words as "my aching back!" and such.

If you are facing a physical challenge and someone asks, "How are you?" instead of responding with an "organ recital," let something good be said! You can say that you know that you are in the flow of life and that you are getting stronger every day. Or if you are on the verge of saying something negative about yourself, or wanting to pass on a choice bit of gossip, let something good be said!

There may be a time when you yearn for some word of Truth from a counselor or teacher, some specific answer to your need. Actually, you may more importantly need the contagion of a triumphant spirit. In a Sunday worship service, you may not receive the answer to your need in so many words, but you may experience a heightened consciousness in which you will unfold your own answer. It is the finest way, the only unfailing way.

Take a moment right now to get into the vibration of your own inner sanctuary. Be very still. Let your heart sing its song of joy. As the cells of your body clap their hands in ecstasy, your whole being is now synchronized with the rhythm of the universe. You are now ready to go forth into your world with the healing, harmonizing, and projecting vibration going before you to make safe, joyous, and successful your way.

## The Truth About Direct Knowing

Everywhere there is a professed need for guidance: for children, for marriages, for business. Yet if someone publicly suggests that he depends on divine guidance, he may be looked upon with distrust. Often it is seen to be mystical or some kind of magic.

There is an almost instinctive feeling in every person that there is something beyond his personal prejudices, something more than his worries, something that *can* be reached. However, all too often this something has been dealt with on the level of superstition: the flip of a coin, tarot cards, tea leaves, stars, or a crystal ball.

We witness fantastic evidences of guidance in nature, and we call it instinct. But if a person has such an experience, we call it ESP or

Spirit guidance. Why do we refuse to accept as fact that: "*... it is the spirit in a man, the breath of the Almighty, that makes him understand*" (Job 32:8)?

Perhaps it is because our religion does not deal with the whole person. We walk alone, unaware that we are all One. We live in a field of infinite knowingness, but we are deaf to the process. Emerson says: *There is guidance for each of us, and by lowly listening we shall hear the right word.*

We need to expand our thought of God to a real awareness of omnipresence, to know that the whole of Spirit is present in its entirety at every point in space at the same time. There is no distance between God and man. There is nowhere to go to get guidance. We are in it all the time.

The expression, "voice of God," is misleading. When Moses heard God speak in the burning bush, it was a knowing so clear that it was as if God was speaking to him. He was told to take off his shoes, meaning to let go of preconceived notions and to become as a little child.

Jesus said: "*... your Father knows what you need before you ask him*" (Matt. 6:8). God is present, and God knows. Knowing is, and it is at hand. It is now. The way out of the problem is at hand. But this knowing comes only to the uncluttered mind. If you know *about* a lot of things, it is difficult to know the Truth, to know the Knower.

A creative person may be so involved in knowing that he lets go of what he knows about, even if it may indicate impossibility. True creativity flows when the mind is unrestrained by a knowledge of the facts, for direct knowing transcends facts.

Few persons experience direct knowing in their prayer efforts because they are preoccupied with preconceived notions that they bring with them into their prayer time. The mind that is cluttered with images and goals successfully frustrates the process of direct knowing.

The highest form of prayer is not reaching for things but accepting allness. It is to "be still and know" that Spirit is present as the Presence. The answer to your dilemma is present, here and now. There is nowhere to go, nothing to reach for, no one to contact or plead with. For that would imply absence, and direct knowing is Presence.

When we hear of instances of direct knowing, we tend to write them off as chance or special revelation or psychic intervention. Actually, many of our hunches and leadings evidence direct knowing. We need to have more faith in the guidance process. For the presence of God, the activity of the Holy Spirit is always present where we are. It knows our needs and is constantly seeking to bring them into fulfillment.

There are not really thousands of things to learn in life. There is only one thing to learn: to know the Knower within and to acknowledge Him in all our ways. This is to understand the superconscious level of mind, to learn how to get and keep in the flow of guidance. Wherever you are and however urgent may be your needs, you can be still and know that you are in the flow. You will experience an effusion of light in the form of creative ideas, unerring guidance, and answers without ceasing.

## The Unconditioned Power

There is a great need in the world today for a religion that is practical and livable. We need a philosophy that leads us to a sense of unity with the Infinite and with the infinite number of human personalities with whom we live and do business. We need a concept that leads to the release of our innate potential for wholeness of mind and body, serenity of spirit, happy and prosperous living, and for the creative fulfillment of the persons we are intended to become. Actually, we need go no further *than* the teachings of Jesus, but we must go further *with* these teachings.

Many persons have gotten caught up in worship of the man, Jesus. Some Christian sects have emphasized the divinity of Jesus, while Jesus Himself taught the divinity of man. He clearly demonstrated that the power of God is limitless, and He taught that man is endowed with this power by which he can do all things.

Jesus clearly distinguished between God-power and the power of the human: "... *the Son can do nothing of his own accord...*" (John 5:19). "... *the Father who dwells in me does his works*" (John 14:10). He did say, "*All authority in heaven and on earth has been given to me*" (Matt. 28:18). But lest we think this indicates a special dispensation of God-power, He also said: "... *he who believes in me will also do the works that I do...*" (John 14:12). All power is given to every person. However, though we may be the channels for great spiritual creativity, we should never say, "This is my work." There is only one true power, and that is God, who works in us, creates through us, and manifests as us.

The power of God is infinitely greater than the instrument through which it expresses. Of itself it is unconditioned. The conditioning element is our faith, our attitudes. People of supposed limitations have displayed phenomenal power in times of crisis, doing things that appear to be contrary to the laws and limitations of their physical condition. Mushrooms are known to lift a pavement several inches from the ground, and oak trees have grown through solid granite. The power inherent in all nature is unconditioned and can unconditionally meet all the special requirements of man or the world of nature around him.

Hearing of amazing accomplishments of someone, often we say or think: "That is all well and good for him. He is a genius; I am just an ordinary person." This is the reason for our so-called mediocrity. So we condition the power as to just fill our self-image and expectancy.

Sam Walter Foss points this out in his poem, "Confessions of a Lunkhead." He tells of a country boy who is a self-styled "lunkhead and lummox" who is puzzled over the fact that other young men, not knowing that they are also lunkheads, go out and become governors, army generals, and multimillionaires. He reasons: *Where would I be if I didn't know I am a lunkhead? I might be settin' in the presidential chair.* As long as we continue to think of ourselves as average or limited, we will continue to condition the God-power that dwells in us.

Paul gives us the key to appropriating this

great power when he says we should be "absent from the body and present with the Lord." This means that when our minds dwell on the human and its limited resources, we can only do certain limited things, and we appear to have no strength in reserve. But when we are "absent from the body," when we get our minds off the problems and obstacles, and focused on God, the unconditioned power that dwells in us, nothing will be impossible to us.

*There is only one Presence and one Power, God, the good omnipotent.* This is a staggering statement when we really comprehend its meaning. Power, God-power, is with you and in you every moment. Whenever you turn your thoughts to God, you become one with power without limit.

## The Whole in the Part

The British High Command was once
studying some areas of military involvement
in a distant place on the globe. The War
Minister stepped back and said "Gentlemen,
we need larger maps." To consider the subject of healing in the broadest possible context, we need to enlarge our frame of reference. We need "larger maps."

Most of us have grown up under the influence of a religious philosophy that dealt with
a universe of many parts: God and heaven
above, Earth and human life beneath, and
hell and satan under the Earth. We may have
gained freedom from the latter, and we may
have changed our view to an "omni" perspective of the former (omnipresent, omniscient,
and so on). But so often we have failed to

really "get it all together."

We may think of God *in* man, God *guiding* man, God *protecting* man, but it is still God *and* man. In this consciousness prayer is a kind of negotiation with God, and healing is something that a helpful God does for us. Thus we reveal that, though we have the new insight in Truth, we may well be putting *"new wine into old wineskins."*

Jesus said: *"I and the Father are one."* It is a giant idea that has been obscured because people have thought that Jesus' relationship with God was unique with Him. Actually Jesus was saying, "You live in the universe, and you are a part within the whole. But the whole of things is also within you, and there can never be a separation."

*Holy Spirit* is a common term in Christianity that is rarely understood. Ministers talk about it as a divine personality that comes and goes by grace or divine whim. Here is an idea that, if you once grasp its full import, will lift you to a new high awareness that you will never again lose:

*Wherever Spirit is at all, the whole of Spirit must be. And because God or Spirit is omnipresent, the whole of Spirit (Holy Spirit) must be present in its en-*

*tirety at every point in space and time.*

This is a fantastic concept! No wonder it has not been widely understood in religion. Be sure, as a student of Truth, that you understand it. It is the foundation on which the whole structure of your consciousness of Truth is built.

What it means is that God in man is the Holy Spirit or the whole of Spirit. The whole of Divine Mind, the whole of divine love, the whole of infinite substance is in you and in focus as you at every moment in time, wherever you may be. *Wherever I am God is* in His entirety.

Whatever else we may ultimately find the universe to be, it is whole. We may not see or understand the whole, even the whole at the point where we exist. But it is whole, and in that we can feel secure. Nothing can be taken out of the universe, and thus nothing is irrelevant or inconsequential in it. This means that you are important. You are whole!

Your life may have many phases, your experience may reveal many conflicts, but you are a whole creature. There is always that part of you that transcends any experience of illness, lack, or inharmony. Note that I said, "That part *of* you, not that part *in* you." The idea of Spirit *in* man is often thought of as something added on, like a shadow. Spirit *in* you *is* you. You are Spirit. It is the whole of you which you may be expressing in part.

This concept of the whole in the part has been sensed by biologists seeking to understand the miracle of growth in plants. Edmund Sinnott refers to something present in the plant that represents *the natural configuration of the whole.* This could very well be the plant kingdom's counterpart to Paul's "Christ in you." The seed can become the tree because the tree is in the seed. You can become what you desire to be because the Christ, your divine potential, is within you. It *is* you. Whatever is, is whole, whether or not you can see or experience that wholeness.

Seeing wholeness is not easy because of the influence of the emotions, the senses, and the intellect. From partial experience we judge by appearances. But when we "judge righteous judgment" or see wholly, we see one-to-one. This is really what that lovely Hindustani word *namaskar* is all about. The whole of me salutes and relates to the whole of you. It is seeing oneself or others as we *can* be.

Politicians are wont to say, "We are living in troubled times." But the great mystic teachers have always taught the presence of transcendent power. *"In the world you have tribulation; but be of good cheer, I have overcome the world"* (John 16:33). This is to say that the problem exists chiefly in our own minds, and the way out is in the allness of Divine Mind within.

Today there is a great interest in human potential. This is good! Unfortunately, the application often suggests putting something into us, conditioning the subconscious mind with new power and ability. Human potential is divine potential. God can never be more than God nor less than God. Man, created in God's image, can never be more than that God-pattern within, nor less than it. It is a matter of realizing potentialities, not adding to but opening out a way.

Thus, your potential is not something you can perhaps achieve. It is a reality even before you begin to work for it. It is the whole of you which you may be expressing only in part. It is that of you that is always whole, even if the surface self may be ill, confused, or in poverty. Everyone has the desire for health, for success, and for a life-affirming existence. But the desire has a cosmic origin. It is the part sensing the whole. You could not desire healing if you were not already whole.

The word *possibility* comes from the Latin *posse,* which means "to be able." This calls for the affirmation *I am able.* Declare this, not to put something into your mind, but to get into the flow of the creative process. The health you want is now yours, because you are now whole. The love you hunger for is within you now because you are now a limitless expression of divine love. The wisdom you seek is within the depths of your mind now, for you are now an expression of Divine Mind minding your mind. When you "treat" for help or healing, or use the affirmative approach in prayer, it is not a means of creating something, waving a magic wand to bring your good out of the ethers. The affirmation, as the word implies, adds firmness to your consciousness of wholeness.

The old hymn sings, "Holy, Holy, Holy." It is usually reserved for a church service. Actually, it is a dynamic projection of spiritual power if one remembers the true meaning of "holy" as being "whole." Singing or saying, "Holy, Holy, Holy" can be a sense of relating to life (seeing or sensing it) from the perception of wholeness. It is a commitment to see

wholeness everywhere—in persons, relationships, the economy, world affairs—and in
oneself.

## Did You Make the Grade?

In the month of June, a time of tests and graduations, the question is repeatedly asked, "Did you make the grade?" Did you pass the examination, get the scholarship, or move on to the next grade? While this is a major concern for many young people, it has a distinct application in the lives of all of us.

There is a lesson to be learned in every experience. When we have a series of challenges to meet, what happens to us in the process of meeting them is much more important than why they happen. We can go through an experience or grow through it. The choice is always ours. But one thing is certain: if we simply go through the experience, we may well find ourselves going through similar things again and again. However, if we grow through the experience, we graduate to a higher level of understanding and of living.

When the Israelites finally went into their Promised Land, all the forty years of wandering in the wilderness became worthwhile. For it was during that time that they progressed in consciousness and experience to the point where they were ready to "enter in and possess the land."

We are living in a time of great turmoil. The institutions and values of yesterday are being challenged—and changed, sometimes by evolution and sometimes by revolution. We may be wondering, "Where will it all end? What is the world coming to?" Perhaps only a seer or historian can say. But in terms of day-to-day living the question is irrelevant. More important is how you are meeting the challenges and changes. Are you anxious and troubled and fearful and pessimistic and bitter? Or are you singing with the old hymn: *Everywhere change and decay I see, O thou who changest not, abide with me?*

The student of this new insight in Truth should always seek to find the inner side of everything. As long as we think of challenging experiences as problems, we will see them as hopeless situations we must endure. The word *problem* has dark meanings: a perplexing question, situation, or person. A matter involving difficulty in solving, settling, or handling (such as solving the problem of inflation, military conflicts, and the spread of crime). When we think of world or personal problems, we identify them with difficulty of solving, settling, or handling. A better word would be *project*. Every seeming problem is simply a project through which to externalize the spiritual idea. The word *project* connotes a positive endeavor of research or development. We tackle the project of landing a man on the moon with vigor and imagination, and with the conviction that it will be done. But we tend to deal with the "problems" of war and poverty as if we were just going through the motions in situations that are hopeless.

Take a look at your life. How many projects can you find? (You used to call them problems, remember?) Give them priority for your attention, and then get busy applying yourself to them one by one. You will have to work and grow. But isn't that what life is all about? Life is a school, which means that there are not only lessons to be learned in the everyday challenges we meet, but there is the "boning up" for the tests, for education in

61

spiritual things. James Hilton's character Mr. Chips was once disturbed by a parent who said, "After my son finishes his education he will enter my business." Mr. Chips exclaimed "Good heavens, does the fellow think education is like the measles—something you get over while you're young so that you don't have to be bothered with it ever afterward?"

To paraphase Jesus, "The tests are plentiful but the students are few." There have always been multitudes on the sidelines, crying, "What is the world coming to?" The world calls for those who make the grade by working for solutions that begin with themselves. Jesus fittingly said: "... *when I am lifted up from the earth, (I) will draw all men to myself*" (John 12:32).

## The God Spell in You

The Bible is an outline of the principle and the process of spiritual evolution, with Jesus symbolizing the final stage. Contrary to tradition, Jesus was not God becoming man but man becoming God, man feeling the upward pull of the Divine within him, and, through discipline and overcoming, going all the way to mastery. That Jesus did it is good news, for thus it is a reachable goal.

The word *gospel* literally means "God spell." Jesus taught and demonstrated that every person is a spiritual being with the built-in potentialities of the kingdom within, and with *"the Father's good pleasure"* to unfold and express them. It is a divine ferment, an ascending urge, an upward pull. It is the God spell that explains Jesus and ennobles the human race.

The central point in the Gospel stories is not Jesus but the Christ Spirit that He discovered as the principle and process of the fully functioning life. When Paul referred to *Christ in you, your hope of glory,* he wasn't referring to Jesus but to the dimension of divinity. This is the good news—not that Jesus alone was divine, but that all persons are inherently divine.

Of course, you may have a long way to go in this spiritual evolution. But the good news is that you have something going for you. There is a God spell upon you. It is like the upward pull of the sun on the sunflower that causes the blossom to open and face the sun. This doesn't mean that God is "up there." The up is *in.*

Jesus demonstrated and taught that every person is an *eachness* within the allness of God, an integral part of a dynamic universe. It has been said, *you can trust a universe that creates flowers.* And you can trust a universe that has made you, for it has made you in and of itself. You are the focus of an infinite idea. Within you is the divine pattern of what you can be, and the gentle urge to press on in the high calling of God.

When you catch this idea of the God spell, you will realize that divine Sonship is not the projection into you of something unlike you. God cannot project Himself out of Himself; God can only *be* God. You are not an individual *in* God, but a unique individualization *of* God, with the divine ferment, the God spell all wrapped within and inseparable from you.

It is an exciting concept, for it means that, though you may have been struggling to achieve or acquire something, within yourself you already have it. Stop trying to "get it," just "let it!" Relax, let go of tension, stress, and strain. Know your oneness in God. Feel the life, substance, and intelligence of God streaming into you from all sides. Dwell in the glorious feeling that the universe is involved in you as nature is in a flower. It is the ceaseless longing of the Creator to fulfill its divine pattern of the Christ in and as you.

Take heart! The whole universe is on your side. You can achieve! You can succeed! You can overcome! This is what the Bible says. This is what Jesus is about.

## The Tall and the Small

The great problem in working with children is not with them but with ourselves. We think of them as creatures that must be pushed and pulled, that should never do anything wrong. They are people in the process of growing up even as we are growing up. We must recognize that most of our troubles with children come not from their infancy or adolescence but from our own immature reactions to them.

There are no lost children, no bad children—only untaught, misguided children. The responsibility of the "tall" is to guide and direct the "small". But we can only do this when we remember that they are people in a different stage of development than ourselves. Every individual, tall or small, has within him the God-given power to do what needs to be done, and we can help our children by expecting them to express that inner power. But we must patiently allow for their development. When we hastily say, "you naughty child," naughtiness may consist in the fact that the child is simply involved in the difficult experience of being age three or nine or a teenager.

We often talk about the "depraved generation" of young people. Our youth today are more involved and concerned, and also more mature and insightful, than any young generation in history. We tend sometimes to see unusual hairstyles and dress as proof of depravity, but these things may be simply evidence of an important resurgence of individuality. The vast majority of our young people are good and normal. Sometimes they're reckless, lacking a sense of responsibility, maybe clumsy and boisterous, but young people have always acted like young people.

*Our youth now love luxury. They have bad manners, contempt for authority, disrespect for older people. Children nowadays are tyrants. They no longer rise when their elders enter the room. They contradict their parents, chatter before company, gobble their food,*

67

*and tyrannize their teachers.* Surprisingly, this was written by Socrates in the fifth century B.C. Writers have always expressed concern for the "modern generation of young people." Maybe when we are tall we forget that we, too, were once small.

We do have a responsibility to guide and discipline our children. But we teach more by example than by precept. Often the major influence on our children is our thoughts about them. We must see them as children of God, not "little demons." Children are God's great possibilities. But when we hold negative thoughts about them, we are God's great problem. We stand in God's way by our insistence on holding the thought that a child is naughty or wayward. The first step in changing the child is to change our thoughts about him.

The child will make mistakes and we must correct him. When we discover a bad or wicked act, we should not show disapproval of the child, but only of the act. The act may well be wrong and might harm him or others. But he is innately a good child who simply needs to express his goodness. You can never make your child "be good." He is good. Your role is to help him act like the good child he is.

Parents often feel that children absorb their lives. If this is true it is their fault. The child can't understand what it means to be a parent unless we help him to understand that we, too, need time to relax and play, time to grow and develop. Children will understand this if parents are humble enough to admit it to their children. Parents should take time to do the things needed to grow. In the end they will be more respected and appreciated by the children when the family becomes a happy fellowship in the common awareness that, tall or small, we are all involved in the common project of growing up.

## There Are No Miracles

The repeated emphasis of the word *miracle* among new thought thinkers saddens me. It is completely at odds with the implication of Jesus' teaching. You may also be surprised to discover that the title of this piece is a direct quote from Charles Fillmore, indicating that we can't blame the trend on him.

A miracle usually connotes a supernatural happening, a setting aside of natural law. To talk about miracles, to encourage their expectancy is a kind of spiritual naivete, relating to a universe of caprice. Fillmore says that the use of the word *miracle* is an attempt to excuse our ignorance of divine law. Referring to the increase of the widow's oil, he says: *This was not a miracle—that is, it was not a divine intervention supplanting natural law—but*

*the exploitation of a law not ordinarily under-
stood. Jesus used the same dynamic power
... and five thousand people were fed.*

Commenting on the fact that emphasis in
Bible study is normally on the miracles
wrought by the prophets, Fillmore says:
*... all over this land enough demonstrations
of the supermind are taking place every day
to fill many books of the size of the Bible....
there is a restorative law that, if taken advan-
tage of, will heal the world of all its ills....
these demonstrations ... are still looked upon
as miracles, notwithstanding the fact that
logic and science shout from the housetops
the universality of law.... God never per-
forms miracles.... Whatever the prophets
did was done by the operation of laws inherent in Being and open to the discovery and
demonstration of every man.*

This in no way means that we should debunk the amazing power to heal and trans-
form. On the contrary, we should have
greater faith in this power. Yet, we need to
come to grips with the idea that divine power
is natural power at the level of man's divinity. All things are possible, not because God
makes an exception for you by reason of your
pleas, but because your faith is a key to the

kingdom of the power within you to apply the laws that transcend human limitation.

Fillmore says: *The universe was not created through illogical assumptions of law. Law is its foundation. There are no miracles in science. Jesus did no miracles. All His marvelous works were done under laws that we may learn and use as He did.*

Reject the idea that you should look for magic, for some divine sleight-of-hand to reach into your life and bring about changes. It is nice to enjoy good luck, but the belief in luck at all opens the way for the possibility of bad luck. The expect-a-miracle approach builds on the idea of the lucky turn of fortune. The new science of prayer is not a naive effort to coax a miracle from a reticent God, but a commitment to be transformed by the renewing of the mind, along with a conviction of worthiness wherein one may claim his good as a child of God. The result may *appear* to be miraculous, for amazing things can and will happen. However, it is simply the fulfillment of divine law.

To talk of miracles is to limit demonstration to the whim or caprice of an external force. How much better it would be to rejoice in the infinite possibilities inherent in you, the allness of God expressing as you. The healing you long for, the overcoming you desire, the manifestation of prosperity and success for which you have been praying so fervently, do not call for a miracle. They call for the disciplined application of divine law and the steady effort to know God.

## Be a Center of Love

When the world around you is in turmoil,
you may be confused as to where you should
stand. When social issues become polarized
and politicized, people may demand to know,
"Are you for us or against us?" It is important to know that you need not become
trapped in divisiveness. You can take a stand
for unity. The one thing to be against is the
tendency to react in anger and hostility, to
give vent to feelings of bias and prejudice.
And the important thing to be for is the way
of love.

You can be a positive onlooker. A referee or
negotiator plays an important role in many
disputes. It is not a passive or weak-willed
function. His is a dynamic activity even
though he takes no stand for or against. Any-

one can become an arbiter of good feelings, a center of love.

Edwin Markham reveals a dynamic formula:

> *He drew a circle that shut me out,*
> *Heretic, rebel, a thing to flout;*
> *But love and I had the wit to win,*
> *We drew a circle that took him in.*

You may have been shut out by people; nations and ideologies may have erected barriers. But in the new age one must have the wit to draw a larger circle of love to include and bless persons and groups of persons. If you are surrounded by any kind of conflict, don't slip into the black-and-white concept of right and wrong. When you become judgmental, no matter what you say you stand for, you are on the side of the problem. Instead, be an active onlooker. Dissolve your concern in a time of quiet meditation, and then, in your mind's eye, draw a circle around the whole scene, including yourself. All parties, all sides, will come into your sanctuary of consciousness. Here you will easily overwhelm them with a love that will dissolve differences and open the way to understanding communication.

This is an extremely important insight for

the student of Truth, especially as it pertains to politics and preelection rhetoric. Don't stop short in dealing with issues by taking merely a political stand. Certainly a vote on issues is your democratic responsibility. However, a consciousness of transcendence is your spiritual responsibility. Become an arbiter of peace. Bless all persons and all parties. Meditate on the idea that you are a channel for the expression of the infinite love of God. Feel a flowing forth of love going out in all directions to bless all persons everywhere.

The world needs the radiation of your love; but don't delude yourself that the world needs your religion. Don't become a proselytizer, a missionary zealot for Truth. The world needs unity, not theology. Many persons have accepted Truth through their emotions, and thus all your logic or scriptural or scientific authority will be of little avail. It is useless to appeal to a person's mind if his mind has had no part shaping the convictions to which he so tenaciously holds. Many persons think that the practice of Truth is in passing out pamphlets on the street, or in crassly voicing metaphysical platitudes in a completely unreceptive conversational group. There is a better way. Be a "meta-missionary," dealing with seeing things or people right instead of the misguided effort to set them right.

Certainly the message is universally needed. But as far as you are concerned the great need is to change your consciousness, dissolve your prejudices, and heal your fears. The Truth is for you! It is a practical process by which you can achieve an effective life and at the same time become an effective instrument of love and harmony.

The missionary supports his effort by the Gospel teaching: *"Go into all the world and preach the gospel..."* (Mark 16:15). However, Jesus also said: *"I, when I am lifted up... will draw all men to myself"* (John 12:32). For the meta-missionary the charge is clear—go into the world of your own consciousness to convert the errant states of your own mind. Having done this, you are ready to go into the world to preach the gospel, but you will be a center of love, and your influence will be more in what you are than in what you say.

Become a center of love. You will become a positive influence in your community. But more important, you will be centered in a circle of protection. In this awareness, no harm can befall you, for anyone coming into your space is lifted into the aura of your consciousness.

You can become a center of love. Enough centers of love in the city and around the nation will help to evoke wise actions by our government, and bring the unified support of the people. Enough centers of love around the world will build bridges of communication and peace. Love is the answer.

## The Twain Shall Meet

In Genesis there is a metaphysical story of the descendents of Noah journeying to the East, where they found a plain and dwelt there. Modern Bible scholars indicate that this is a mistranslation. It should be: "The people journeyed *from* the East . . . ." Symbolically, *East* refers to the inner, the spiritual, the divine. *West* refers to the outer, the material, sensual, and worldly. Thus, the sons of Noah journeying from the East means they were falling from their spiritual roots and setting materialistic goals. Here they began to build the Tower of Babel. The word *babel* means "confusion." When we move from the East, when we lose our base of spiritual awareness, we set up causes that result in division and confusion.

There is a much-used cliché, "East is East and West is West, and never the twain shall meet." It has been used to support all kinds of prejudice. Actually, it is from a poem by Rudyard Kipling, taken totally out of context. The poem says:

*Oh, East is East, and West is West, and
never the twain shall meet,
Till Earth and sky stand presently at
God's great Judgment Seat;
But there is neither East nor West,
Border nor Breed nor Birth,
When two strong men stand face to face,
though they come from the ends of
the earth!*

In other words, the twain *shall* meet when two strong people stand face to face.

There is a common tendency to deal simplistically with people in terms of good or bad. Prejudice points to certain groups of people as "they." "They should be stopped . . ." or "They can't be trusted." We need to return to the insight of Truth, return to the East. For in Truth, all persons are sons of God. Everyone is both Eastern and Western, divine and human. East and West are not just geographical and social groupings. They are two possibilities that every person carries within himself or herself.

Paul says: *And we all, with unveiled face, beholding the glory of the Lord, are being changed into his likeness from one degree of glory to another . . .* (II Cor. 3:18). The veiled face symbolizes separation. The unveiled face is what Kipling has in mind when he refers to two strong people standing face to face: a communion of Spirit, nothing hidden, open and free. Paul says *that we all may be one.* This means to be a whole person, balanced, integrated, disciplined. Only out of this personal wholeness can we find true communication with others.

We may think we will be *one* when we find the kind of people with whom we can relate easily. But it is not in finding the right person, but in finding ourselves. To be *one* is to be whole, to know ourselves as spiritual beings, moving easily in the world of human relationships but always guided by Spirit. When we are in the flow of life, we no longer see in a mirror darkly, but face to face.

When we journey from the East the tone of our lives is completely set from the outside. And when looking for excuses, we cite things "out there" as the problem. We are always on the defensive. Anyone has the power to make us angry or upset.

Note how a person in a dark room bumps into things as he fumbles for the light switch. Then when he touches the switch, the room is flooded with light. He doesn't change anything in the room, but suddenly it is changed. This is why the time to salute the divinity in someone is at the very moment when you are tempted to make the opposite appraisal. You are moving from the East. Jesus says to turn the other cheek. He means get yourself straight, face to face, so you won't be looking out of the corner of your eye or talking out of the corner of your mouth. Let the Christ in you relate to the Christ in the other person. Suddenly there is a light in your eyes and a response of light in his.

If you treat an alcoholic as a weak person or an ex-convict as a criminal not to be trusted, you block any effective communication. But if you face the person with unveiled face, see him as if the unborn possibility of his divine Self were already present, you will find yourself pushing all the right buttons, and he will begin doing things he has never done but always wished he could do.

When you journey back to the East, your attitudes will change. People will seem to change, and they will deal with you differently because you will be different. You will feel the flow of the peace that passes understanding in and through your life. A radiance of peace will go out from you into the world to help the whole of humankind come a little closer to oneness. Yes, the twain of East and West shall meet when you find your oneness within yourself.

## Suddenly It Is Spring!

After a long winter, it is good to witness the springtime pageant. Through the forests and meadows, across farms and gardens, spring has touched the earth with a gentle hand and warmed it with a sweet breath. New life is in evidence, color has returned, the pulse beat of people and nature is stronger, and everywhere men and women are taking up their daily tasks with lighter hearts.

Walt Whitman refers to the *ever-returning spring*. I think he means, not the annual occurrence of summer-fall-winter-spring, but rather the eternal evolving of that which is involved, the constancy of growth and renewal. Could it be that the season of buds is really the autumn, because behind the old leaf that falls, the new leaf is safely embedded? It is there even before that. The tree never really stops budding.

When a blind person demonstrates an amazing sense of touch, this sharpened sense was not given to him to compensate for what he had lost. The sense of touch had always been there, long before the young man had to use it as he does. That same sense is present in every living person. Biologists claim it to be the oldest of the senses.

We refer to a great musician or artist as gifted, as if his talents were handed to him on a silver platter. Certainly, he may have definite talent. But its masterful development involves recognition, discipline, and practice, practice, practice. Occasionally a critic announces the discovery of a new genius in the field of the arts. But the chances are that long before he was a genius he was a struggling student. More than this, what the genius demonstrates is what man *can* do. A Shakespeare and a Beethoven ennoble the whole, showing the potential of the entire human race.

All that you can be, you are now. You cannot become a spiritual being, or become a child of God, because you have always been these; you have never been anything else.

You may close the door on your inheritance as the man who can see and hear closes the door on his wonderful sense of touch. But his closing the door does not mean that he no longer has this sense. Jesus tried to urge people to awaken from the slumber of their cosmic capacities when He asked: *"Having eyes do you not see, and having ears do you not hear?"* (Mark 8:18). A development such as that observed in Edgar Cayce does not indicate a unique faculty, but a unique awakening to a universally inherent faculty.

Of course we look for times of sowing and reaping in accordance with the Earth's seasons. But within the apple pit is the image of the tree, the blossoms, and other pits! Naturally, we do not expect the apple first and the blossom after, but we know for certain that both are there within that tiny pit. We know it has only to "open its door."

Divine inheritance is not something you have to attain, but a growth-unfoldment to be awakened and released. This is truly what Easter is all about. Thus, spring is not some set time on the calendar. It is the open door to the Earth's inheritance, the everlasting yes to transcendent life. May this year's performance of spring work magic in your life, opening doors and windows of perception and experience. May you come to enjoy a greater awareness of the spring of life which is progressively being awakened and released. And as spring happens in your garden, may Easter happen in your life.

## The Story of Everyman

The great Truth of the ages is *unity*, oneness, as captured in the lovely Jewish Shema, *Hear, O Israel, the Lord our God is One.* In oneness there is health and well-being; in separation in mind from the One are sin and suffering and lack. Jesus said: *"I and the Father are one."* He made it clear that this is the ideal state of everyone. It is a meaningful concept beautifully articulated in Jesus' parable of the Prodigal Son in chapter fifteen of Luke.

It deals with a father and two sons, but it is the story of one person—you. The father does not represent God as a being "out there." Instead he represents the Christ of you, your own permanent identity. The father *is* the son, that which is always stable and dependable, no matter how the human may seem to be scattered.

The younger son represents that of you which is sensual and worldly and materialistic. He is lured out into the "far country," for that is where he thinks the action is. He is deluded in thinking that the way to find himself in life is to have the most sensual experience of life. This represents that of you which is ego-centered, sensation-centered, material-centered. In time he is stripped of his sense of self-worth and meaning in life. And he is cut off from the flow of the creative process. He goes to work after squandering his money.

The Prodigal is reduced to feeding hogs for a living. This symbolizes life at its lowest ebb. It could mean failure and lack in his finances, or it could have been an experience of great success and affluence with a debilitating lack of meaning, a total confusion of his sense of values. Every person may well go through this prodigal stage at some time. Perhaps it is a necessary step in personal growth. Perhaps we must go out into the "far country" so that we can grow back into the consciousness of true oneness.

The parable then says, *he came to himself.*

This does not mean that his problem is over. But it is an important turning point. It has been said that the most important part of learning is unlearning our errors. Of course, first we must admit that they *are errors.* When the alcoholic realizes that he is powerless over alcohol, there is hope for him, and there is help for him. Thus, the Prodigal realizes that his problem is self-induced and can only be solved by self-unfoldment.

Note that the father stands unmoved through all this, symbolizing the stability and ever-availability of the Presence within. If the father had compelled the son to stay at home or to come home when he got in trouble, he would always have remained a prodigal at heart. Only when he "came to himself" was a homecoming back into the feeling of oneness possible. In other words, God can do no more for you than He can do through you. God cannot make you healthy or happy or prosperous unless you let God be God in you.

When the prodigal Son decided to go home, he rehearsed a little speech that he would make to his father: *"Father, I have sinned against heaven and before you. I am no longer worthy to be called your son; treat me as one of your hired servants. "* However, there is a serious flaw in the commitment, which must be corrected before he can experience oneness again.

Recall the story of the Israelites, under the leadership of Moses, seeking their Promised Land. *Egypt* symbolizes bondage to sense and materiality. It was their far country where they had come to know want. Moses represents their coming to themselves. Under his leadership they marched out of bondage across the Red Sea and right to the border of Canaan. Here they sent a reconnaissance group of spies into the land to determine their chances of capturing it. The group returned, saying that there were men of great stature in the land, and . . . they seemed to themselves like grasshoppers, and so they seemed to the giants (Num. 13:33). So they wandered in the wilderness for forty years until they outgrew that grasshopper consciousness.

So the Prodigal Son arrived home. The time lapse could have been forty minutes or it could have been forty years. It is irrelevant. What happened along the way is important, for when the son delivered his prepared speech, he said, *"I have sinned against heaven and before you . . . "* but nothing about becoming a hired servant. He had dropped the grasshopper consciousness. He was suddenly in the flow again, as symbolized by the festive homecoming party the father staged for him. He is given shoes for his feet (representing new understanding), rings for his fingers (representing the consciousness of the authoritative word of Truth), and the best robe (representing a new self-image of worthiness, a feeling of wholeness).

When one turns from separation and embraces his oneness, it would seem that "the very hills clap their hands for joy." When there has been a restriction, there is a block of the flow of good. When the restriction is removed, there is a surging inflow of the essence of life. This homecoming of the Prodigal is descriptive of the experience that comes through meditation when we become inwardly attuned and outwardly radiant.

Now the older brother has stayed home to work faithfully and dutifully in his father's fields. He is not too happy with the treatment received by the younger brother. After all, he reasons jealously, he did not recklessly spend his inheritance, and the father had never thrown a party for him. He represents the conforming part of consciousness which does not break from inner guidance to seek after freedom and worldly experience, but which realizes this inner guide only as a restriction. While he did not go out into the far country, he did go out from a sense of oneness. In his bondage to obligation, he too is in the servant consciousness. By his jealousy he indicates that he is a prodigal at heart and has probably secretly longed to do as the younger brother did, but hasn't had the courage. Behind the facade of respectability there are bitterness and cynicism. Through all the years while he has faithfully served his father, he has secretly resented it. Thus, as the younger son has come to himself, the older son will have to do his own changing. He will have to open his eyes and drop his servant consciousness.

So, the older brother refuses to join the party for the Prodigal Son. In his pouting there is similarity to Martha demanding that Mary come and do some of the work and not just sit at the feet of the Master. On that occasion Jesus said: *"Martha, Martha, you are anxious and troubled about many things; one thing is needful. Mary has chosen the good portion..."* (Luke 10:41-42). This may seem unjust, for in life, the Marys seem to leave all the responsibility to the Marthas.

But again Martha and Mary are two parts of *your* consciousness, as the older and younger sons in the parable symbolize two states of consciousness in you.

The father said to the older brother: *"Son, you are always with me, and all that is mine is yours."* This means that there is always an allness, even within an illness. No matter what your partial experience may be—whether you are experiencing the lack and meaninglessness of your own far country through neglect of your spiritual life, or whether you are allowing your spiritual devotion to become ritualistic, mechanical, and self-righteous, with all the smugness, criticism, and jealousy that such an attitude usually leads to—the father in you, your own Christ life of infinite potential stands ready as your help in every need. Wherever, whenever, and however you come to yourself and lift your consciousness to a new sense of creative "worth-ship," you will experience a renewed flow of the creative process in you in a veritable "eat, drink, and be merry" festivity. This is the story of Everyman.

## The Uncommonsense Way

Common sense has been heralded as a logical and workable philosophy of life, but actually it is the consensus of the known. "Everyone knows that you can't trust people," and "men are all alike." It is this kind of consensus thinking that leads to wars and conflicts of all kinds. One can only see where he has been. Thus, common sense is backward logic.

It is only because people have, from time to time, had the uncommon sense to renounce their past that they have made even halting steps in personal growth. It is only because, as a race, we have been able to transcend our past performances that we have forsaken caves and primitive ways and progressed up the spiral of civilization.

It is said that common sense is of the common man. But the common man is an illusion. Every person is uncommon, unique, individual, with great depths of potential. Whether in medicine or psychiatry, or education or criminology, to deal purely with the common is to totally inhibit the possibility of health or growth or reform. "It is just common sense that some conditions are incurable, some students are ineducable, and some criminals are beyond help," some say. But in every field there have emerged people of commitment who have had the uncommon sense to believe in the divinity of man, and who have done the "impossible" by releasing undreamed-of inner potential.

A young man has failed at every turn in the world of art. He had been told by a number of newspaper editors that his cartoons were inferior and he had no talent for a career in either classic or commercial art. He was reduced to using a mice-infested garage for a studio. He decided to draw the mice in all sorts of situations. It seemed to friends to be a senseless preoccupation to draw pictures of silly mice. They urged him to give it up, for "common sense should tell you that you are on a one-way street to nowhere." He set off for Hollywood, saying, "Common sense is another way of saying fear, and fear usually spells failure." In time the "silly little mice" became Mickey and Minnie Mouse, and Walt Disney went on to become one of the most successful artists in the history of the world.

The commonsense view is the conservative view. "History is what we have been. We can only be what our past performance reveals. The future will only be an extension of the past. Thus we should shore it up, keep in step, and not rock the boat." So says the conservative.

Nowhere is this more true than in religion. Conservative religion is religion in retrospect. The emphasis is on the prophets of antiquity, great historic creeds, and the rites, rituals, and traditions of other times. Emerson, one of the most notorious of uncommonsense thinkers said: *The foregoing generations beheld God and nature face to face; we, through their eyes. Why should not we also enjoy an original revelation to the universe? Why should not we have a poetry and philosophy of insight and not of tradition, and a religion by revelation to us, and not the history of theirs?* In short, why not a presence of God that is present, here and now?

The commonsense forms of religion, liberal

Christianity and liberal Judaism, modify old concepts to fit the mold of human consciousness. This is the big difference between liberal religion and practical Christianity or New Thought. Liberal religion makes the fundamentals more acceptable by watering them down in conformity with consensus views. Practical Christianity renders the ideas in a form that can be understood, and thus practiced. The one circumvents the fundamentals to make them easier to live *with*. The other is catching the spirit of the teaching to make it easier to live *by*.

In the uncommonsense view of Truth, we are not what we have been, but what we can be. Since the mind of the Infinite is within us, we are the mind of the Infinite expressing *as* us and can be all that we can conceive of being. It is common sense to admit to one's weaknesses. But the uncommonsense view is that weaknesses simply conceal strengths. It is common sense to justify insecurity and fear by the appearance of the economy, the tenuous nature of jobs, or the sad balance of your bank account. However, the uncommonsense view is that which Victor Hugo suggests metaphorically: that we be like birds which, pausing in flight awhile on boughs too slight, feel them give way, yet sing, knowing that they have wings.

When we take the uncommonsense view we can deal victoriously with life. We can know that we are made for mastery, for victory, for releasing the unborn possibility of limitless life. Thus, we can keep on, wherever we may be, and whatever may be the challenges. We can know that the goal of life is to *open out a way whence the imprisoned splendor may escape.* For that is the uncommonsense way of life.

## Your Extra Senses

The quest for Truth is set in the framework of many unexplained and unexplainable phenomena. As Walt Whitman says: *We are not all included between our hat and our boots.* We talk of "sending a thought," "expansion of consciousness," and "absent treatment." It becomes obvious that we are involved with areas of perception beyond the five senses.

The frame of reference of primitive man was pretty narrow. He was surrounded by supernatural phenomena, such as lightning and shooting stars and eclipses. As his knowledge of the universe expanded, his supernatural world contracted. By the 19th century, science had summed up the cosmos in a completely mechanistic concept.

The five senses were developed from an

original general sensitivity, much like the sense of touch. Next came taste, a specialization of touch. Then came smell, a refinement of taste. Then a wider world was revealed through hearing and seeing, which enabled man to transcend space and sense things he could not touch. Each of the five senses is a specialization of a primal pervasive psychism or sensitivity. Research now indicates that every one of the billions of cells has the latent potentiality for all the senses, and that, in a very real sense, every person has the potential to relate to the world in various extrasensory ways.

Should we, then, attempt to develop ESP (extrasensory perception)? No! The senses develop in proportion to the need and the consciousness to handle it. They are a means of communication that should be integrated into the whole person in a whole universe. When we get involved in "signs and wonders," titillating ourselves with phenomena, we lose our sense of wholeness, and thus seek to understand what we call "paranormal" things.

The search for paranormal phenomena is normally motivated by a lack of the sense of meaning. It is the search for reality, for

Truth, for God. However, even as the one thing a fish can never find is water, so the one thing man can never find is God. Think about it.

So we go on a merry-go-round of all kinds of phenomena, deluding ourselves that we are on the path. Meaning is found only within ourselves. The need is to see ourselves as an eachness within the allness of the universe. Then, wherever we look, we are simply exploring dimensions of our own greater self. The terms *ESP* and *paranormal* are naive since they reveal a limited awareness of the senses and a higher kind of norm beneath the realization of the whole person.

The student of Truth should resist the allure of the supernatural, for it is a return to primitive insecurity. Plotinus gives us a lofty ideal to reach for when he describes the universe rushing, streaming, pouring into us from all sides, while we stand quiet. When we are at the center, where is there to go? Even such a practice as meditation is not an attempt to find anything, to feel anything, or to get into anything. It is very simply a matter of being still and knowing that "... *it is your Father's good pleasure to give you the kingdom*" (Luke 12:32).

The cause of human problems is over-involvement in sensuality and materiality, the failure to engage seriously in the process of growth. We cannot fill this need by working for psychic promptings. Admittedly these may point to our human potential. But this potential can only develop where there is readiness in consciousness, and then only by means of growth from within-out, not by dabbling with phenomena at the periphery of experience. The purpose of life is to evolve that which is involved, to release our imprisoned splendor, rather than looking for life's answers in some past or future life, or in some exterior psychic influence on this plane. Our greatest need is to get in tune with the upward, progressive sweep of life from within.

Emerson gives a timely challenge: . . . *go alone . . . and dare to love God without mediator or veil. Friends enough you shall find who will hold up to your emulation . . . Saints and Prophets. Thank God for these good men, but say, "I also am a man." . . . cast behind you all conformity . . . live with the privilege of immeasurable mind.*

## *How to Change Others*

The attempt to change people is the greatest energy waste of all, not because people can't change, but because change is a growth process from within. In most cases the desire to change another person arises from the very subtle urge to make him into something he is not. This other soul can never be anything than what he is, though his potential may be seriously frustrated.

It is a perfectly natural thing to see the needs of people and want to do something about them. However, much as you want to change another person, the first step is not to *set* him right, but rather to *see* him rightly. And to see him rightly you must get rid of some very narrow frames of reference. For instance, if you have an enemy, you must get rid of your enmity. If you are very much troubled over the crisis being faced by a loved one, you must first dissolve your troubled thoughts.

All the persons about whom you are concerned, no matter how much you love or hate them, exist (as far as you are concerned) in your mind, your prejudices, your concerns. Though it is certainly possible to be an influence for good in bringing about great changes, the process involves something you do within yourself.

Here are four ways in which you can be an influence through which changes may be effected in the life of someone you are concerned about.

First, pray about the person. It should be noted that much that passes as prayer for a person is little more than concentrated worry about him. Prayer for oneself is a matter of lifting one's consciousness from one level to another. But how can you lift the consciousness of another person? You can't. You can only lift your consciousness, no matter how concerned you are about someone else. And yet you can be a great help. The starting place is your concern. When you rise above this human perspective, you will begin to feel at peace about the person, and then you can whisper a quiet "Namaskar!" to him. This means that the divinity in you salutes and relates to the divinity in him. Feel good about the realization that beyond the appearances there is an allness within his illness, an all-sufficiency within his seeming insufficiency. How long should you pray for this one you want to help? As long as you feel concerned. Whenever there is a feeling of release and inner peace, the work is done.

Second, establish yourself in the conviction of the divinity of man. Practice believing in people. Instead of generalizing about the limitations of people or groups ("You just can't trust people these days"), look for the good performances of people and generalize them ("Aren't people wonderful?"). One of the most effective things a parent can do for a child, a teacher for a student, or an executive for an employee, is to believe in him and let him know that you do.

Third, if you really believe in people, you will find it easy to bless them, and you should do so. When you meet and greet people, when you talk or write to them, let your faith in them flow through a "namaskar" attitude. There are many levels of consciousness in people and in ourselves. We can always make contact with any person on the level in him we choose. If someone rubs us the wrong way, we are probably reacting to him in the abrasive he-makes-my-blood-boil level of consciousness. Obviously there is a conflict. A large portion of the "good life" will open to you like a new horizon of abundant living when you really understand Jesus' turn-the-other-cheek technique. We can't control the actions or behavior of another person, but most certainly we can regulate what we react negatively to. When we discipline ourselves to turn quickly to a higher level of perception, we may be amazed at how rapidly other persons begin to interact with us on the higher level. All people with whom we have communication unknowingly and yet dramatically will begin to act more friendly and loving and harmonious.

Fourth, act as if the change you want to see manifest in another person has already taken place. It will give you a sense of release from the pressures and pain in your relationships. Goethe said, when we take a person as he is we make him worse; but when we take him as if he were already what he should be, we advance him to what he can be. Three dozen words that surpass a whole library of books on human relations. Certainly pray for people, but remember you must change your thought about them. Believe in people. Hold to the awareness that every person is a child of God, no matter how he is acting. Salute the divinity within people, see them and deal with them in the namaskar consciousness. But most importantly, treat them as if they were already what you believe them to be.

Treat the alcoholic as a weak person, or the ex-convict as a criminal, or the young rebel as an outcast, and you prevent any effective communication, creating all kinds of blocks in you and in them. On the other hand, believe in the inherent goodness in the person and treat him as if it were actually there, and you will find yourself pushing all the right buttons in him.

In a very real sense the only way you can change what another person is and does is by changing your thoughts of concern, and by committing him into the Father's keeping.

# Up-to-Par Insurance

*Thou hast given him dominion over the works of thy hands; thou hast put all things under his feet...* (Psalms 8:6). This means you! You were created to be the master of fate and circumstance. Your thoughts do not have to be reactive. You can think the kind of thoughts that you want to see unfolding in your life. You have the capacity to be "up to par," not just occasionally but all the time.

A great fallacy of human thinking is that such things as joy and love and zest for life are simply the effects of good experiences. This is in error. The enthusiastic person does not act in that way because things are going well with him. It is more true that things are going well because he is an enthusiastic person. The happy person does not need something to be happy about. He is happy because he is a happy person. And happy people seem always to attract the kinds of experiences and relationships that justify happiness.

The expression *up to par* originated in England many years ago. There was a man named Thomas Parr who reportedly lived to the age of 152. He became such a legend that "feeling up to par" was an expression of feeling dynamically alive, a kind of keeping up with Thomas Parr. Parr must have had a great desire to live. If there is a desire for life, the health process will find some way to unfold no matter what the age or the medical diagnosis.

One does not lose enthusiasm because he is getting old. He begins to age through the loss of enthusiasm. One can be the victim of advancing years or he can be their master. Dr. Eric Berne wrote that supremely enlightened people use three words in life: "yes," "no," and "wow!" The "wow" expresses a healthy childlike wonder.

The question is, are you willing to take responsibility for your life? We often delude ourselves that our problems are caused by the world. We think we are "down" because of what he did or what they are saying. We say it will be different when things change. Actually, the way we feel has little to do with things or persons, and everything to do with how we may be reacting to them. To get "up" again, we need only to change our thoughts.

Most of the things we get down about are like little pebbles. Hold a pebble close to your eyes and it fills your whole world. Hold it at a proper viewing distance and it can be examined and properly dealt with. Drop the pebble at your feet and it becomes part of the gravel of the path on which you walk.

You can be up to par all the time if you have the desire to be, and if you are willing to stir up the gift of God that is within you. Someone has said, *"Every person contains within himself the wherewithal to surpass himself."* Wherever you are, whatever your problems, and however deep you may be in the morass of depression, you can rise phoenix-like from the ashes of defeat and self-limitation, and recover your equilibrium.

In a very real sense your whole day is conditioned in two five-minute periods: upon awakening in the morning, and just before sleep at night. To insure that we keep up to par in the face of life's exigencies, we need to establish some creative habits of spiritual discipline in these periods.

Prepare yourself for the day by resolving first thing upon awakening that you will face the day with the highest perspective. Take a few minutes for deep breathing, holding the thought that as your lungs are being filled expansively, so your whole being is being filled with the inspiration of the Almighty.

A good drill for relaxation and sleep at night is to think of a compass needle that points north unless it is attracted by some metallic object. Remove that object and the needle returns inexorably to North. This suggests a great thought: you do not have to strain to get close to God. Just let go of anxieties and there is an immediate return to oneness.

You can keep yourself "up to par" for there is that in you that is always in the divine flow. Pause often to remember that God has given you dominion. Keep yourself in the thought of oneness in the divine flow and you will be sustained in a mental, emotional, and physical condition of "par."

You will live deeply, fully, and abundantly. It is the purpose of this new insight in Truth to help you do just this.

## The Quiet and the Strong

We live in an age of speed and accomplishment. We go more places and do more things in less time than seems imaginable. Without a doubt it is the spirit of industry and ingenuity that has made our nation great. But we have come to the critical stage where we must decide whether the machines and high technology we have created are going to master us, or whether we are going to master them and keep ourselves in tune with the rhythm of the universe.

I have come to the conclusion that whenever I feel I have so much to do that it seems impossible to accomplish it all, this is the very time to pause and take a break. To go forward at this point and in this consciousness is not only unwise but dangerous. Whenever we are late, we are out of attunement. Hurry and rush will not reestablish this attunement any more than racing your engine will get your car into gear when it has slipped into neutral. The need is to pause. Get the thought of hurry and its related fear out of mind.

*"In returning and rest you shall be saved; in quietness and in trust shall be your strength"* (Isa. 30:15). Quietness seems to suggest something soft and easy. But it isn't. Quietness is strength. Only the very strong person can be quiet, and only the quiet person can be very strong.

One of the great problems of the industrious, ambitious person is that he crams his life full of every conceivable activity. He prides himself on never having an idle moment. His philosophy is: "Keep busy and get things done; do it now!" Robert Louis Stevenson says: *Extreme busyness, whether at school or college, kirk* (church) *or market, is a symptom of deficient vitality.... It is no good speaking to such folk: they cannot be idle, their nature is not generous enough....* He infers that a bursting display of energy might well camouflage a large spiritual vacuum.

We need to discover the pleasure of pausing. Sometimes when it seems that we must "do it now," it might be wise to do it tomorrow instead. Sometimes the most urgent need in the midst of the feeling of urgency, if we listen to the inner voice, is to pause and relax. Sometimes rush and urgency become so habitual that we cannot really tell whether we rush because we feel things are urgent, or whether we feel things are urgent because of the habit of rush. Many persons even take the habit of rush and hurry along with them on vacations taken for relaxation. They hurry along in the breathless awareness of everything, and a true appreciation of nothing.

The reason we sometimes feel tense about things that must be done is that we are not realizing our inward resources through which they can be done easily and well. We need to "wait on the Lord," to put off doing the thing so as to dispel the tension that results from urgency and let the subconscious mind help us to organize the ideas and solve the problems. Take a moment to return and rest by mentally taking a trip on the magic carpet of imagination to a place in your memory where you have found peace, some beautiful scene that you have witnessed, a cool mountain lake, or a field of golden poppies.

We all need to relearn the art of pausing, the art of doing nothing. We need to make time to sit on a park bench or rocking chair, or to relax in a hot tub, where we can let large clouds of nothingness drift through our minds. In this way we can let our souls catch up with our bodies and get in tune with the rhythm of the universe. Let us give thanks for the consciousness of divine order in our lives, the realization that: *For everything there is a season, and a time for every matter under heaven* (Eccles. 3:1). Then let us resolve that we won't be rushed, and that we won't necessarily do it now.

## Off the Deep End

A great throng of people pressed Jesus close to the shore of the Sea of Galilee. He stepped back into Simon's boat, where from the stern He taught the multitudes the deep things of Spirit. Finally, He said to Simon: *"Put out into the deep and let down your nets for a catch"* (Luke 5:4). Simon objected, saying they had fished all night and had caught nothing. But he did as requested, and the nets soon enclosed a miraculous haul of fish so great that he had to call for help. Soon several boats were filled. This transcendent experience caused Peter (as Jesus called Simon), James, and John to lay down their nets and follow Jesus as disciples.

This turnabout in the lives of the fishermen was so impetuous and drastic that friends probably said, "They have gone off the deep end over this Jesus. Religion has its place, but one need not become a fanatic about it!" Perhaps you can identify with the disciples, for undoubtedly your enthusiasm for Truth has evoked similar reactions from your family or friends. Don't be too disturbed, for if you have been called a fanatic, it could be a backhanded compliment. It comes from a Latin word that means "inspired by divinity."

E. Stanley Jones tells of natives in Malaya who sit all day in rice paddies, fishing in one foot of water even within sound of the breakers of the ocean with its limitless supply of fish. It is a parable of the spiritual experience of so many persons who remain in the shallows of thinking and living, fishing for their spiritual insights in the comfortable pews of formal churches that deal for the most part with "propositional theology."

How great is the need to push out into the deep waters of Spirit. Jesus said all things are possible to those who believe. Do you believe? Enough to step out on the promises? Enough to begin to do the things you have long dreamed of doing? On the wall of the National Library in Washington, D.C., is the inscription: *For a web begun God sends the thread.* What a beautifully revealing thought! There is a limitless potential of wisdom and strength and substance within you, and it unfolds as you take the first step.

How many persons carry their hopes and aspirations buried within them? They are listless, indecisive, and discouraged, with "no hope" written all over their faces. The great Truth is, within you is the unborn possibility of limitless life, and yours is always the privilege of giving birth to it. The need is to get out of the shallows of self-limiting thought and launch out into the depths of limitless Mind.

Most of us, as students of Truth, are "overread and underdone." We must realize that the goal should not be to accumulate metaphysical knowledge. Certainly, in our time of need we may reach out for more Truth. However, as the farmer replied to the salesman of books about scientific farming, "I ain't farming half as good as I know how now." The answer is already within us, as well as the keys to call it forth. The need is to take the first step in the direction of our dreams. God will send the thread, the guidance, the creative ideas, and, yes, even the money.

A young man wanted to be a writer. This is not so unusual, for many persons indulge in thoughts such as, "Someday I am going to write a book!" But for most persons it is an "impossible dream" indulged in while fishing in the shallows of limited thinking. Not so with this young man. He heard the call and put out into the deep. He kept on in the face of those who told him he was "off the deep end," that he would never be able to earn a living. When he did, in fact, establish a writing career, he had a new call to launch out—in search of his "roots." Yes, it was Alex Haley. He spent twelve long years searching in a way that was little short of fanatical. He kept on, and God sent the thread. The best-selling book and the phenomenal response to the television mini-series prove that when one is willing to go off the deep end, he is in a country where he can drill for oil and hit a gusher.

Truth works, but you must work at it. You must be willing to take a stand, follow a commitment, even if people do not understand and call you a dreamer. It may be making a career change, going back to school, or working on a healing need by prayerful means against the advice of doctors and friends. There is no limit to what you can do or be if you have the courage to launch out into the depths of spiritual thinking.

In your quest for Truth, don't stop short with simply being entertained or pacified by peace-of-mind platitudes. Truth should disturb you, challenge you deeply. It should ignite sparks within you, set fires under you, stir up your enthusiasm. It should lead you to release your inner power by which you can become a more creative and successful person. You can awaken your potential for limitless life that may have been lying dormant for years. Only as you go off the deep end will you find the real depths of your life.

## Mysticism for Moderns

It has long been held by the mystic teachers of the world that all great work has been done by the Spirit. Too much stress has been laid on brainpower. The brain has been thought of as a great cauldron in which ideas are generated out of nothing, as it were.

This great country had its genesis in ideas that were divinely inspired. During the framing of the Constitution, the delegates were bogged down in a complete impasse. Someone suggested that they pause and seek the guidance of the one Mind in which all ideas inhere. History records that, following that prayer, the Constitution came forth as if it were being divinely dictated.

The dictionary defines *mysticism* as the *doctrine of an immediate spiritual intuition of*

*truths believed to transcend ordinary under-
standings, or of a direct, intimate union of the
soul with the Divinity through contemplation
and love.* Actually, the mystic is one who
really believes that he lives and moves and
has his being in God.

However, mysticism and psychism are not
the same. Communion in psychic realms may
lead to revelations of Truth, but there is
always the danger that it may lead to confusion and conflict. On the other hand, the
mystic union with the Spirit of God within
leads unfailingly to the inspiration of the
Almighty that gives understanding.

The mystic does not read human thought,
but rather he sees the atmosphere of God.
Mystics are people like Jakob Böhme, an
ordinary cobbler, who looked up and saw the
soul of God in a geranium plant, and people
like Moses reading God's law from a burning
bush.

Note, however, that the terms *mystic* and
*mysticism* are purely relative terms. As with
the term *hi-fi,* some equipment has a higher
fidelity than others, so some persons or experiences may be more mystical than others.
Every student of Truth who seeks to practice
the Presence of God is a mystic in the sense

that he is working for the consciousness that his life and its regulation come out of the divine flow. The inner prayer that I outline in this new insight in Truth is a mystic practice.

There are undoubtedly people in business who appear to be wholly immersed in materialism, who are intuitively guided in most major decisions. They may not be conscious of any mystic union of their minds with God-Mind, or that they use spiritual power at all. But we can see it in the quality of their work and the unerring caliber of their decisions.

There is nothing peculiar or fanatical about one who has found this mystic union. It is simply the full functioning of the whole person. You may have felt this inner guidance or intuitive flow often. It is nothing to be ashamed of. Acknowledge it freely and give thanks for it. Stir up the faith to believe that in all things you are in the divine flow to guide your hands, direct your footsteps, and put the words into your mouth.

Press on in your study of Truth to an ever greater awareness of oneness with God. You are not separated from life, neither is life separated from you. You are a separate and individualized center in God. But with the realization of the mystic union let us not degrade the intellect or human skill. Let us pray and work, think and feel, and unify ourselves with the unseen guide and apply ourselves in wisdom and good judgment. This is mysticism for moderns.

## The Meaning of Grace

Few words in Christian theology are used more or understood less than *grace*. What does it mean? How does it work in our lives? Though this word has been wrapped in mystery, it is really a very simple explanation of the natural flow of the creative process in the individual.

Why are you favored as a child of God? Simply because you are God expressing Himself as you. Why is your hand favored as a part of your body? Because it is your body expressing as a hand. Thus, the hand not only has strength but also feeling and tenderness.

*God's will* is another confused religious term, the understanding of which will help us to understand grace. The will of God is the ceaseless longing of the creator to fulfill Himself in and as that which He has created. This will or creative intention is so great that it even seeps through one's willfully closed mind. You could declare, "I wish I were dead!" Yet, despite the power of the spoken word, you will go right on living. Why? Because God's will for life transcends even an occasional human desire for death. This is grace.

Grace explains the inadequacy of the idea of "karma," the endless cycle of cause and effect. It is true that "as you sow so do you reap." Yet, God's desire to express completely through you and as you is so great that you never completely reap the harvest of error, and you always reap more good than you sow. This is grace.

You are not a helpless creature bobbing about like a cork on the seas of life. You are the very self-livingness of God. When you desire spiritual growth it is God who first desires it in you. When you make an extra effort in your work, it is the divine urge in you that is working through you. You are not simply a subject of God, with God making notations of sin and error, or of good and righteousness. You are the activity of God in expression, beloved with an everlasting love.

The law of consciousness is inviolable. The high consciousness heals, and the low consciousness weakens. However, something of the infinite is always filtering through and becoming part of your consciousness. Thus, the most sordid or limited thought is modified by God's love in you. It is like living in a house with every window and door tightly closed. Invariably, there is enough air leaking in around the windows and doors so that your oxygen needs are met. This is grace.

Grace, as the divine favor, the activity of God's love, is working for you constantly. It is not dependent upon any special faith or prayer on your part. Like the buoyancy of water that will keep you afloat even when you try to force yourself under, so grace fulfills divine law in terms of sustaining you in spite of yourself.

You do not have to earn grace. It is not something that comes only to the good. It comes to all alike, simply because all alike are expressions of God. By the grace of God, a criminal is still loved by God and can find forgiveness and ultimate rehabilitation through an activity of love that transcends law.

Grace is simply an explanation of a wonderful facet of the activity of God in you. It is not something to work for, to develop. It simply is. It is an assurance, an explanation of why things are never quite hopeless, and why we never quite receive the full harvest of the error we sow, and why we always receive a little more good than we sow.

It is a beautiful and meaningful word, but when you hear, "He was healed by God's grace," don't forget that it is not a special act of God for one person, but a specialization of the divine "good pleasure" that is in every person.

## The Changing and the Changeless

It is not difficult to answer the question, "What is Truth?" But it is difficult for most minds to understand the answer. Truth is not simply the total of one's metaphysical concepts. Truth is infinite and immeasurable, like the universe of which man is constantly expanding his knowledge. Truth cannot be captured in a school of thought. It is an ultimate.

Michel Eyquem de Montaigne once wrote: *We are born to inquire after Truth. It belongs to a greater power to possess it.* No one can know the whole Truth, not even the greatest mystic or master. To know Truth's allness would be to become speechless, for Truth in its absolute sense is incommunicable. To claim that you have found the absolute

Truth, or even the perfect path to absolute Truth, is to delude yourself and announce to the world that you are forsaking the quest.

Truth is the underlying changeless reality of the universe. There is an inner and an outer side to everything. Truth is the key to the inner side. It is the inner side. We tend sometimes to rest content with the outer side, to live at the circumference of our being and to judge people and circumstances by appearances. Righteous judgment reveals that everything in the outer is but a symbol of that which constitutes its inner being. On the inner side, no matter what the outer appears to be, we find God, we find good.

Prayer is the contemplation of life beyond appearances, the other side, the changeless reality. However, we do not change God by our prayers to Him. He is the great changeless essence of all that is. It would appear that through our prayer God becomes more responsive to us, but actually we simply accept more of that which is. We simply let more of the changeless influence the changing, and thus bring about more changes that we call healing and overcoming.

Orthodox religion has held as Truth the belief that man is an incorrigible sinner. This great untruth has canceled out the positive value of such religion. Sin is simply the concealment of man's son-of-God self. The sin is the changing experience, the failure to express the whole, the divine potential, the changeless reality.

In Truth, in the reality behind every appearance, there is only good. If this is true, then what about the error we see? If I put four oranges and three apples in my bag, and erroneously, by mistake or dishonesty, represent the bag as containing eight pieces of fruit, I am simply concealing the Truth that there are only seven. The error never really existed in Truth, only in thought and the influence of thought.

I may act in an evil manner and do evil things, but I am not really evil. I am simply concealing my goodness. A child with dirt from ear to ear is not a dirty little child. He is simply a child with a dirty face. This is not just a play on words. It is a vital realization. If I am innately evil, I can't change. But if I am a good person concealing my goodness through evil ways, then if I know the Truth, I can be free, I can be healed. There is a changeless reality of God or of good at the heart of every person.

In the same sense, sickness or lack do not exist in God, in the changeless reality of life, any more than wrong answers exist in the principle of mathematics. If God is all, and man has a need, it would appear that we should subtract the need from the resource. That is the way it is done in arithmetic. But in Truth the process is reversed. God cannot fill lack, and (startling as it sounds) God does not heal sickness. God *is* substance, and God *is* life. God is changeless. Our need is to draw the changeless out of the changing, to draw the God-potential out of the person, to draw life out of sickness, to draw courage out of fear. God is not a person outside of us who fills our needs from the outside. He is a dynamic potential within, who fills our needs from the inside. God is always where we are and what we need.

God is not a person who must be flattered or cajoled. He is principle, "closer than breathing and nearer than hands and feet." He is more personal and more available to us than the personal God we believed in yesterday. However, as principle God is never depleted or overburdened. It takes no more effort for God-life to animate every person in the world than it does to give life to one new-born baby. Even as we do not tax the principle to add two plus two and get four, or deplete the power of gravity by dropping a book, so we do not exhaust life by living, consume substance by spending, nor dissipate ideas by putting them into action.

## The Prayer That Never Fails

Prayer is the most misunderstood subject
in the field of religious practice. It is looked
upon as an attempt to coax a miracle from a
reluctant God, a court of last resort. And
there is a tendency to try to see God through
our troubles. "How can I believe in God after
all this?" some say. The real need is to begin
with the idea that God is the whole, no matter
what we see in part. Thus, though experiences change for better or worse, we know
there is that which changes not—the one
Presence and Power of God. We begin with
this awareness and see our troubles from this
consciousness.

This is a kind of prayer that never fails, because we are not looking for miracles, only for
perception. The goal is not to set things right,

but to see them rightly. When we see with this insight, we are in the flow of guidance and strength and love, in the process of the outworking of the problem.

The Sanskrit word for prayer, *pal-al*, literally means "judging oneself to be wondrously made." Prayer is not a means of arousing God to action, but the process of waking up from our drowsiness so we can see ourselves, not *in a mirror darkly* but *face-to-face*. It is knowing that we are created in God's image-likeness with the flow of infinite possibilities eager to come into expression in and through and as us.

Much prayer is directed to God. Its tone is that of reminding God that He is supposed to be Almighty, and urging Him to come to our aid. We don't have to tell electricity to be energy, or gravity to hold things in their places. We begin with these inexorable forces and change our position in relation to them. Where does God come in, then? God does not come in, for He never went out. God is not only *in* all, God *is* all.

Prayer is not a means of reaching God or seeking help from God. For the thought of prayer and the mind that prays *is* God. Prayer is our response to the activity of God that knows our needs even before we ask, and whose will it is to give us the kingdom. As the weather vane does not make the north wind blow, but simply indicates that it is blowing, so prayer does not move God, but it evidences that we are being moved by the activity of God which is constant.

The emphasis in prayer has been on words that are repeated by mechanical repetition. We "say our prayers" out or up to God. But when we understand the wholeness of life and that God is that wholeness, we do not seek to pray *to* God. We know that we are individualizations of God who is all, and we begin at the point of that knowing. We let go and know our oneness, our wholeness—praying, not to God, but from the consciousness of God.

Prayer, then, is a projection of this consciousness of God, speaking the word of Truth. This is the prayer that never fails. For we do not have to make Truth real. It is a changeless reality. We do not have to make it work, for Truth demonstrates itself. Knowing the Truth is not rehearsing affirmations to make God work, for the activity of God is always working. Affirmations do not need to be repeated to make them true. Behind the appearance that may show a frustration of it, there is always wholeness. The affirmation deals with this wholeness. We may fail to grasp it, to open ourselves to the flow of its expression, but the whole is always present. The kingdom of God is within.

The ageless formula of creation is, "Let there be," not "there must be, I wish there could be, dear Lord, make there be!" Just "let there be!" No strain or hurry or force of will. In Genesis we can't imagine any resistance in the elements to the clear command. When we say, "Let there be," it is the full focus of our consciousness saying yes to the activity of God.

This is the simplest and most effective prayer treatment. Certainly, *do your best to present yourself to God as one approved...* (II Tim. 2:15). Certainly, get the mind stayed on that which is spiritually true. But finally "make an end to prayer" and simply accept. What better way than: *Let there be health; let there be substance; let there be harmony in place of discord, joy in place of sorrow, courage instead of fear.*

That which you desire God desires in and through you. That which you work for is seeking you. Stop trying to make money, and let substance flow. Stop trying to make a demonstration, and seek to discover the decision that infinite Mind is revealing in you. "Let there be . . . ." This is the prayer that never fails.

# What Are You Saying to Yourself?

In Mark 5 there is an account of a woman who was instantly healed of a long-standing condition of hemorrhage. Seeing Jesus passing by, she rose from her bed and rushed out toward the throng. She said: *"If I touch even his garments, I shall be made well"* (Mark 5:28). The miracle healing may have obscured the fact that her faith was generated by what she said.

Each of us lives in a world of his own choosing, a world of consciousness. Many things happen around and to you, but the only things that count for much are the things we say to ourselves about what has happened. Every day of your life the world tells you many things, much of it is of the hearsay or "they say" variety: "At your age, you must expect to have aches . . .' '; "They say the economy is due for a slump . . ."; "Everyone tells me it is foolish to hope . . . ." But what are you saying to yourself?

You cannot get away from yourself no matter where you go. You are always environed by yourself, horizoned by your mentality, encircled by your ideas, and constantly influenced by what you say. If your thought is narrow, you live in a narrow world. If your thinking is sordid, cold, and unsympathetic, you cannot enjoy the broader world others live in. . . . *as he thinketh in his heart, so is he* (Prov. 23:7 A.V.). What you think and say determines the life you experience.

A Truth student with heavy responsibilities felt pressed for time. She had developed a habit of saying, "Oh, I just wish I had a time to do nothing but read and study my Truth literature in quiet leisure." Not long afterward, she had a serious fall, and thus incapacitated, she had an abundance of time to read all the books in her library. To her credit, however, when she realized the power of her self-suggestion, she set about to correct the influence. She began telling herself that she was one with the perfect healing life of God, renewed quickly and completely. Her doctor kept insisting that she would be inactive for many months, but within a week she was back on her feet, giving thanks for the lesson in the value of telling herself the Truth.

A good illustration of self-suggestion concerns "hurt" feelings. Someone says or does something that you resent and you say, "He hurt my feelings." Actually, he didn't hurt you at all. What happened was that you said to yourself, "I don't like that and I am going to be hurt about it." And the hurt remained as long as you kept telling yourself to be hurt. It is also true physically, in terms of pain.

A little girl had fallen from her bicycle, badly skinning her knee. She sat on the ground rubbing the sore but enduring the pain without a whimper. A man who saw the accident asked if he could help. The little girl said, "Oh, I'm all right!" "But how," she was asked, "do you keep from crying?" She replied, "I just say to myself, 'Stop that!' and make myself mind me." And there you have the key. We must learn to discipline ourselves in the things we say to ourselves. We should say only what we want to become a reality in our lives and not what we are resisting or resenting. We need to form the habit of having quiet talks with ourselves, to jack ourselves up when we might otherwise be depressed or lack drive.

It is almost frightening to discover how many broken records of self-limitation we play for ourselves: harping on the same old tune of inadequacy, lack of opportunities, parental mistreatment, etc. Try this experiment. The next time you are distressed or discouraged by things and you find yourself playing the old tune of self-limitation, stop what you are doing and get out of the room for a few minutes. Take a walk or in some way get away from the atmosphere. In a frank person-to-person talk, say to yourself, "Now, you are not acting like the child of God that you really are. Get rid of that broken record. You are not the limited creature you are making yourself out to be, but a child of God with the potential to be what you want to be. Let the dead past bury its own. Face forward in the assurance that you can do what you need to do and be what you want to be through the power of your own indwelling Christ."

There is no fate or destiny which puts one person down and another up. *"It is not in our stars, but in ourselves, that we are underlings."* The inferior person is the person who tells himself that he is inferior, and who insists upon the inferior position because he thinks the best is intended for others. This is utter nonsense! Good belongs to the person who qualifies for it by right of consciousness.

The person who forms the habit of rejecting the "they say" evidence of the world and who keeps telling himself things that are constructive has solved one of the great riddles of life. When tempted to slip into the "slough of despond," tell yourself, "Stop that! You are a radiant, all-wise, all-loving, all-conquering child of God." Don't worry about what others say or what appearances seem to be. What are you saying to yourself?

# Dynamic Lent: A New Insight

Every year in late February or early March the Lenten season begins. It is, or can be, a marvelous experience in self-improvement. In a way, Lent is coincidental with spring, the season of new growth in nature. The trees and flowers are not content with the fruitage of last year. And if we are in the flow of the creative process, we experience divine discontent, in which we feel both the possibility and the need for growth.

Lent is traditionally a forty-day period of piety and discipline. It may be a sincere commitment to the spiritual life, but it is more often a superficial attempt to assuage the conscience with a show of repentance. However, Lent can be a dynamic experience if it is approached with the will toward honest self-examination, self-discipline, and self-commitment.

Whether or not you follow the ecclesiastical observance of Lent, consider its metaphysical application. Turn from the simple act of giving up things to a more positive commitment to *take up* the practice of high-level thinking.

For instance, Lent is often a discipline to give up certain foods. This is somewhat like dieting. Unfortunately, if one holds onto a self-image of "too fat," his practice is self-defeating. Try a new approach. Don't give up anything. Instead take up a new image of yourself. "Think thin," and you will find yourself eating less and more wisely. And your weight will balance itself more effectively than when you tried so hard to give up things.

If you must give up something, give up the tendency to consider yourself weak and undisciplined. The smoker often says, "I would like to quit, but I am just too weak." Get some altitude in your thinking. Emphasize *I can* instead of *I can't; I will* instead of *I wish I could.*

Emerson refers to prayer as *the contemplation of the facts of life from the highest point of view.* It is a great idea. Form the habit of reaching for the highest point of view in all your dealings. It is a way to pray without ceasing. Take up this practice and you will worry less about what to give up.

If you have been letting things get you down, take up the idea that you are the master of your thought world. No matter what people do or say, no matter what may happen around or to you, take up the idea, "Why should I let these things determine how I am going to think or act?" Keep the spirit of joy, the attitude of gratitude, in good times and in bad.

Take up the practice of speaking the positive word, "Let something good be said!" Commit yourself to a diet of words that are positive and loving. Whether you are talking to or about people, events, or ideas, let something good be said!

Lent can be a dynamic experience, not by what you give up as much as by what you take up. More than just trying to lose weight, you will be working to shift the weight of your consciousness from the negative to the positive and creative. It can be a time of great believing leading to great overcoming and great living.

# Get Rid of Your Crutches

Excessive dependency is a common ailment. It may be in the form of leaning on friends, teachers, doctors, or ministers. Or it may be a dependency on alcohol, cigarettes, coffee, or drugs. We have been misled with the belief that we come into life as empty creatures who must find fulfillment in the world. Unless something happens within us that reveals our relationship to the divine flow, we look for sure harbors, strong arms, and all kinds of synthetic means of support.

We need to know that... *he who is in you is greater than he who is in the world* (I John 4:4), so we can overcome any situation or meet any experience without leaning on people or stimulants. We must work at it. We must grow. Growth is what life is all about.

Take a careful inventory of your behavior. You may note that you are too easy on yourself, that you give in too quickly. For this reason you discover and use only a small part of your potential. Challenge yourself to go a little further, beyond the point of weakness. Reach for God before reaching for the aspirin bottle. Try a brief meditation before giving in to the medication. Pass a meal when you realize that you are being ruled by the dinner bell. Take time to realize your inner support before you run home to "mama" (lean too much on a friend or advisor).

This is not a morality judgment. Excessive dependency is sinful only in the sense that sin is the frustration of your potential. Every time you "over-lean" on anything or anyone other than the strength of the Almighty within you, you progressively lose your self-respect.

You can get rid of your crutches, but first you must be willing to change your thinking. You can't rise to new strength while dwelling on your weaknesses. Begin seeing yourself in the light of the possibility of change. Don't fall back on the cliché, "That's just the way I am."

Thought is always parent to the act. You

may have been starting with external facts, and thus you have created a repetition of facts of a similar nature. Now reverse the process. Start with Truth. Think the kind of thoughts that will produce the kind of conditions you want to see manifest in your life. Know that you are created in God's image-likeness with limitless potential to do and do well all that needs to be done.

You may have accepted weakness as the starting point: "After all, I AM only human." But you are not only human. You are human *and* divine, and the divine is enclosed in the shell of the human. Like the egg in the nest, you must hatch out—and you can. Weakness is habitual because your thought about yourself has been habitually negative. There is no such thing as inherent weakness, only deep-seated subconscious patterns of limitation. But "underneath are the everlasting arms." Strength is the reality of you. It is the divine level with which you need to identify whenever you are tempted to lean.

You can be free, you can overcome, you can get rid of any and all crutches—not by will-power but by the outforming process of consciousness. It is not will but willingness. God wills it! Say yes to it!

## The Midpoint in Eternity

"Happy New Year!" It is a lovely senti-
ment, but the fact is, the new year will bring
little that is different for you unless you arc
different. Each day of the year the sun will
rise and life will go on, with things unfolding
as you expect them to and as you create them
through your levels of consciousness.

And yet this year is a very special year, for
it is the midpoint in eternity. You can start
here and go back into the dim past or forward
into the limitless future. You can start where
you are and build on your past experience.
You can go forward into the future to achieve
anything you can conceive and believe.

It is wise to take a brief look into the past
year, not in regret or resistance to change,
but with the commitment to form right

thoughts about every experience. You can't have the year back to set things right, but you can begin now to see them rightly, and find beautiful release and freedom.

Resolve to let go of backward-looking consciousness. Note the expressions: back to work, back to school, back to normal. These words imply monotony and unhappiness. Never go back to anything! Go forward to the new adventures that each day holds for you. Life is an ongoing adventure. Let the new year be a time of reaching forward with eagerness and anticipation.

In the coming year resolve that you will develop the art of looking forward with faith. Many persons look forward in resigned expectation to more of the same, or squint forward, seeking a prophetic glimpse of a predestined future. In this latter sense one is fair game for all sorts of negative astrological or psychological pronouncements.

The great thing, according to Carlyle, is *not to see what lies dimly at a distance, but to do what lies clearly at hand.* Determine that, in the days and months ahead, you will live each day as if it were the only day of eternity. Then go forward into each day in faith that you are at the midpoint of eternity, and at the center of life, of the universe, and of God. Know that you can never get outside the circle of the divine process that ceaselessly rushes and streams and pours into you from all sides. Walk forward by faith and not by sight—not in the passive "what will be will be," but in the conviction that life is consciousness.

One of the most beautiful affirmations of Truth is: *Wherever I am God is.* In the coming year, wherever you may be in time or space, God is with you. Another meaningful idea is the realization that: *Wherever I am, I AM.* In January or June, or in April or December, I am! It is the one sure thing about the year to come: I am!

Each day of the year work with skill and knowledge and foresight. Go as far as you can go and do as much as you can do, and then put your hand into the hand of God (know your own I *am*). It shall be to you better than light and safer than a known way.

What will the new year hold for you? Don't waste time trying to look ahead. Instead look within to that in you that is the midpoint of eternity. *Vaya con Dios!* Go with God! It is the most important year of your life, the midpoint between all that you have been and all that you can and will become. Happy new awakening to your potential! Happy new release of your imprisoned splendor! Happy new *you!*

# A Good "Forgettery" for You

Have you ever wished for a good memory?
Do you know that memory is natural to the
mind and that inability to remember is an in-
dication that we remember too much rather
than too little? A memory specialist asked a
statesman if he would like to enroll in a
memory course. The man replied, "Ah, rather
teach me the art of forgetting!"

More important than learning how to recall
things is finding ways to forget things that
clutter the mind. To hold onto hurts, bitterness, and regrets is to persist in ingesting
poison into the system. As Paul says: . . . *do
not let the sun go down on your anger . . .*
(Eph. 4:26). Before going to sleep at night,
empty your consciousness of unwanted
things, even as you empty your pockets. Run

the contents of your mind through a "positive detector." Whatever comes out unjustified or harmful to yourself or others, let it go. By the law of substitution, turn the experience over and see the good in persons and events, and then let it all go.

Perhaps you are harboring a sense of guilt for something done or left undone in the past. Your past is retained only by your thought. It is not the incident but the memory of it that causes the effects of it today. The moment it is dropped from your consciousness it is gone from the only place it ever existed. This doesn't bespeak license, but liberty, freedom from the bondage of the past to which you have bound yourself. True forgiveness, perhaps the only kind of forgiveness, is self-forgiveness. God forgives as you forget and forgive, as you rise above the limited consciousness and walk on.

What you have been is not important. All that counts in your life is what you are reaching for, what you are becoming.

If we throw a log of oak wood on the fire, its entire past as acorn, tree, and log must go in order that the heat and light of fire may take place. If today is to be fired with enthusiasm and the heat of creative action, the past must be consumed. Let go, face forward, and walk on. You can't have the present the way you want it and have unpleasant memories of bygone times too. It is one or the other.

If you are hoping and praying for some new unfoldment, some inner or outer change, are you ready to let go of the person you have been so you can let the flow of unfoldment be fulfilled through you as the person you desire to be, the person God sees you as being? Jesus said: "... *you will know the truth, and the truth will make you free*" (John 8:32). He meant free from the mistakes of the past and the effects of those mistakes. To know the Truth is to let go of untruths. Recalling negatives about yourself is rattling skeletons in your mental closet. They have no reality, but they can stir up great fears.

Life is much more positive, more productive, and far happier on a past-is-forgotten basis. Memory courses are good and helpful, but most of us have more need of learning to forget. We should not try to get fulfillment from past successes nor be bound by past failures. Consider people such as Lincoln, Churchill, and Edison. They respected their minds too much to clutter them with thoughts of failure or bitterness. They had good "forgetteries."

So if there be any virtue or praise, think on these things, file them in the memory mind, but forget the rest. Develop a good forgettery and you will find yourself with an amazingly good memory too, for the two conditions are indissolubly linked.

# *Making Decisions the Easy Way*

*Multitudes in the valley of decision!* Fortunes have been lost, opportunities passed up, chances for happiness gone glimmering, and minds left seething with unrest because many individuals have not schooled themselves in the fine art of making up their minds.

Life demands that you make decisions about many things every day. Some are of little consequence, but others can affect the course of your life. Indecision comes from fear. We are afraid to make the wrong move, to do the wrong thing, to say the wrong word. Also, procrastination is closely related to the "sin" of indecision. We put off making a decision and thus put off action until that tomorrow that never comes.

159

You can learn to make decisions easily. You have had hunches or flashes of insight. This is simply the activity of divine intelligence in you, that in you which always knows, filtering through your own blocked mind. You may have been too involved in human thoughts, too worried, too tense. It is quite possible to have "hunches to order," when we accept their validity and make our minds receptive to guidance.

There are two chief problems that keep us from accepting and following the inner guidance of intuition: (1) We do not have clearly defined goals. Too often we live like a child in a toy store: grabbing one thing, only to throw it aside as soon as we glimpse something else which we think we might like better. Right or wrong, set a course, have a plan. (2) We may have a bad habit of not carrying through to completion action that has been chosen. When you start something, always see it through to completion. Be a bold starter and a determined finisher.

Prayer is the key to right decisions, but prayer can be an excuse for procrastination if we stand waiting for Spirit to move us. Prayer leads to confidence of unity with infinite Mind. But we must still make the choice, take the step. You may stand at the crossroads, praying for guidance as to which road to take, but eventually, no matter what you think or feel, you must take a step in one way or another.

Prayer, then, must serve to remind you of the Christ Mind, your potential genius within. Through the Christ Mind you can make decisions, know right solutions. Affirm: *The Mind in me, being the Mind of God, knows what it wants to do, when it wants to do it, and does it. There is nothing in me that can deter or be afraid of meeting the issues of life exactly as they are.*

Here is a proven technique for making decisions: (1) Get the facts. Often we are in such a muddle that we are not really clear what we are trying to decide upon. (2) Affirm that you have the ability, through the mind of the Infinite in you, to make a right decision. It is your responsibility, your response to God's ability. (3) Realize that God knows, and God is in you. Therefore, within you, you know. Affirm: *I know what to do.* (4) Lay it aside for an incubation period. Put it out of mind entirely. Don't discuss it with people or ask advice. Give yourself a deadline, "At two o'clock on Friday afternoon I will decide."

This is important to discipline and mobilize the subconscious forces within you. (5) At the appointed hour, act as if the decision were already made. Launch forward. Make a decision. Choose a course of action. Do something. Have faith that God is guiding your hands, directing your footsteps, and putting words of Truth in your mouth.

*"Before they call I will answer"* (Isa. 65:24). The answer exists in God-Mind even before we are aware of a need. This is divine law. When you have a decision to make, know that through your oneness with infinite Mind the answer is already there, and that as you make your contact, it will come. If you keep a goal before you, and build the habit of expecting to finish what you start, you will find the decisions will be easier because you will expect to make them. You will not be thinking "maybe it will go away." Follow the five steps until they become routine. You will learn to make decisions the easy way, and they will be the right ones.

Affirm for yourself: *I express the positive power of the Christ Mind in wisdom, love, and good judgment.*

# The Lure of the Impossible

I once heard a minister comment on Jesus' statement: "... *be perfect, as your heavenly Father is perfect*" (Matt. 5:48). He said, "Jesus was challenging man with unattainable goals, with the lure of the impossible. He knew that we had better have goals that are beyond our grasp or 'what's a heaven for?' " Unfortunately, this totally negates Jesus' teaching of the limitless potential of man through His God-self.

As a poet so eloquently put it: *A fierce unrest seethes at the core of all existing things. It was the eager wish to soar that gave the gods their wings.* What is this unrest? It is the basic law of the universe in which everything must continually grow, expand, and develop. Some call it evolution; others call it

God.

The feats of man have often defied logical explanation. From the dramas of Shakespeare to the landing on the moon, we are forever brought face-to-face with the impossible that is accomplished. Evolution is actually the story of the lure of the impossible. Man has achieved his present stage of development because of his congenital inability to adapt to his environment. His whole history is the story of the impossible becoming possible, and the illogical becoming real.

There is a factor of us that can only be explained by the term "self-transcendence." By this innate force we can transcend ourselves, our limitations, our weaknesses, our past. It is true that we have always had war and immorality, but what we are to become we do not yet know.

How we judge and limit ourselves by past experience! Denying the power of self-transcendence, we settle into an "I can't" consciousness that seems completely logical. "I can't because I never have"; "I can't because I am weak"; "I can't because I am too old." I can't, I can't, I can't!

The Israelites feared to enter their Promised Land for there were giants in the land.

Only Joshua and Caleb felt the lure of the impossible: *"Let us go up at once, and occupy it; for we are well able to overcome it"* (Num. 13:30). Man's achievements have always been made by the Joshuas and Calebs. They have said, "The difficult is easy, the impossible will take some time." How often we have problems we cannot solve, wants we cannot cure, and sins we cannot master! We long to realize with Walt Whitman: *Oh, while I live, to be the ruler of life, not a slave; to meet life as a powerful conqueror . . . .*

Humans are evolving spiritual beings. That which is impossible today will be accomplished by someone sometime. Claim for yourself the ideal of the innate and ultimate perfection of humankind and then start where you are to move along the way of your own unfoldment. Keep on and keep on keeping on! The logical-thinking part of you may say, "It is impossible." Listen deeply to the voice of self-transcendence which says, "God is, I am, and therefore I can."

You can, if you refuse to be cowed by the giants of impossibility and follow the guidance of the creative urge within you. As the stately oak tree is in the acorn, so the perfect person is within the person you now are. You may not achieve your goal overnight, but the principle is exact: There is an allness within every illness, there is an all-sufficiency within every insufficiency, and there is the fullness of the Christ within every person. Don't settle for anything less!

# The Needful Emancipation

Today there is much talk about freedom and equality of opportunity for people of all races, nationalities, and religions. But there is an area of need that is rarely considered— "the needful emancipation." Without it there can never be integration of races, compatibility of nations, or peace among men.

In the allegory of creation we read: *God said, "Let us make man in our image..."* (Gen. 1:26). God is a Father-Mother principle. Man, created in the image of God, must have the essence of the male and female principle in him: *"... male and female he created them"* (Gen. 1:27).

When we speak of God as love, we refer to the Mother aspect of divine law. When we speak of God as wisdom, we refer to the

167

Father aspect. In us, love is a feminine attribute, and intelligence is a masculine attribute. As whole beings we are masculine and feminine, and a well-adjusted life demands a balance between the two. When God said, *"It is not good that the man should be alone..."* (Gen. 2:18), this means it is not good for intelligence to act alone. It must be joined and balanced with love if harmony is to be brought forth, thus, wisdom will be expressed. The creation of Eve signifies a refining process through which man brings forth his divine feminine nature.

The most needful emancipation in the world today is to release the divine feminine to balance the activity of the masculine. It is the masculine quality of intellect that has brought forth the age of science, computers that can serve or enslave, nuclear fission that can be a blessing or a curse. *"... Whatever you get, get insight"* (Prov. 4:7). With all our marvelous developments, we must release the balancing elements of love and faith and feeling. Man has often released his masculine qualities to develop great governments and mighty armies, but no nation has ever long endured without a corresponding release of the divine feminine in its people.

This is not to imply that the world's problems are made by men, and that if men acted more like women we would have peace. We are referring to the need for the release of the divine feminine as the balancing factor in both men and women. In fact there is as great a need for the emancipation of the divine feminine in women as in men. In seeking equality, many women have forsaken their femininity to compete with men in a masculine way in the world, thus becoming aggressive and intellectual and unfeeling.

As long as there is a spark of life within us, the infinite love of God, the mother-principle, is within us as the key to fulfillment. We may be successful without love. We might even be healthy without love for a time. But we cannot be whole without love, and thus we cannot be happy or peaceful or fulfilled. In every relationship, every business deal, every group project or conference, the switch marked "love" must be turned on. Men need to realize that being a man means more than proving strength, will, intellect, and "macho." It also means expressing feeling, understanding, and love. Women should remember that being a woman involves the responsibility to lead the way in her life and in the world by releasing the balance of the love influence.

One of the great blessings of marriage is that two people merge the predominance of the masculine and the predominance of the feminine into one union. The result can be (should be) a balanced expression of love and intelligence, of prayer and action, of faith and works. However, every individual can and must release this same balanced expression of love and intelligence in a wholeness of divine activity in his or her own life.

The missing link in the affairs of people and nations today can only be bridged by the activity of the divine feminine. There is a great need for the universal emancipation of the qualities of love and forgiveness and kindness and patience and faith and prayer. Declare your freedom by affirming: *I am a whole creature in God. I walk and work in wisdom and good judgment, and I now let God's perfect love have its way in and through me. With this balance of love and wisdom, I am an integrated expression of the activity of God. I am free and relaxed and successful. I am a radiating center of peace and harmony in the world.*

## Think Yourself Thin!

Let's talk about diet and reducing. Why do we experience the nagging hunger for food? What controls our appetite? The answer is really very simple: our mental state, our consciousness. When you crave certain foods, it is because your mental attitude has created a demand for the food that will make your body reflect the image of yourself in consciousness. You have a certain impression of yourself subconsciously, and the food you eat is used by your body cells to sustain that subconscious image. These body cells are by nature willing servants of the mind.

It is for this reason that dieting seldom produces the desired results. You may starve yourself and lose a few reluctant pounds. But if your self-image is "too stout," you will eventually give in to your appetite and eat what you crave, thus becoming as stout as ever. The craving for food is but the mind faithfully working to outpicture the image in mind. Thin people usually do not eat enough of the fat-producing elements. They are not attracted to them, and actually may dislike them.

What frustrations are experienced by the person who is trying to reduce! He tries "reducing pills," fad diets, and "blitz diets," he misses meals and starves himself to lose a pound or two, which he quickly regains when he returns to his normal diet. Life is one constant struggle with himself and his uncontrollable hungers. He never eats a bite of food without thinking, "This will make me fat." He is always hungry. He is always thinking about food, and the more he thinks the hungrier he becomes. The more he denies himself certain foods, the more they become an obsession with him. And although he tries to reduce, he holds a mental image of excess weight, and the body works faithfully to reproduce his mental image, creating the desire and hunger and craving for the very foods which will create and sustain the larger bulk.

Diets notwithstanding, your thoughts create your condition. How can we lose weight and achieve the beauty and symmetry and youthfulness of body that we desire? *Think thin!* When you are thinking fat, the craving for rich foods only increases as you eat them. But when you think thin, the craving disappears. Think thin and when you eat you will have a satisfied feeling for a normal length of time. Think thin and you will find that you can take your thoughts off food completely. Think thin and you will find yourself eating less than you did when you tried so hard to do without. You can think yourself thin!

Here is a treatment that you might use as a mental diet. Take this spiritual food into your consciousness each day and within three weeks you will forget about the problem of weight: *I am a strong, confident, disciplined child of God. I am established today in the awareness that my body is the temple of the living God. All the functions of my body are harmonized, and every organ is doing its perfect work in a perfect way. I am receptive and responsible this day to divine intelligence within me which knows the needs of my body temple. I will eat sensibly, exercise regularly, and rest sufficiently. I am free from hidden hungers that might lead to excess in eating or drinking. God's love deep within me satisfies my longing heart and fills my soul and body with all that they require to make my life full and complete. My appetite and assimilation of food are in divine order, and my body manifests the symmetry and perfection of God whose expression I am. I see myself in the mirror of Truth, beholding the perfect, ideal form and shape that I desire to express in my body. I see myself thin and healthy and satisfied. Today I will think thin!*

# Love: The One Creative Force

*Some day, perhaps soon, mankind will learn what individuals have always known: that love is the only true creative force in the world.* These are the words of Pitirm Sorokin, the late founder of the Center for Creative Altruism at Harvard University. Here was a man who went through two of the harshest periods in history; those immediately before and after the Russian revolution. He was a man who had every reason to hate, but who said: *The thing I remember most about those days was love.*

He tells of one simple yet amazing experience. He was attending school in a nearby village, walking to school through the snow, with his toes showing through the holes in his boots. The teacher was a gaunt young man who had no reason to give special thought to this son of a traveling painter who would disappear one morning as suddenly as he had come. But the teacher looked at the lad's torn shoes and without a word went to the closet and took out his second pair of boots. "But you," Sorokin said, "what will you wear?" "Keep them," the teacher replied, "Why should I have two pairs when you have none?"

Sorokin said it was this incident that gave him hope for the world today. We are living in another era of violence and hate, and yet, because of what he has seen and of the love that is always to be found coming from people in the midst of the deepest troubles, he had high hopes for the world of our day. Surely, it is love that has always brought out the best in people.

More than a quarter-century ago, a college professor had his sociology class go into the worst slum area in Baltimore and get case histories of 200 young boys. When the students returned, the professor asked them to write at the bottom of each case history the boy's future. Without exception, the students wrote, "He hasn't got a chance." Twenty-five years later another sociology professor came across the study and decided to follow it up. He told his students about the questionnaires and asked them to find out what had happened to the boys. The students did so. With the exception of twenty boys who had moved away or died, the students learned that 176 of the remaining 180 had achieved more than ordinary success as lawyers, doctors, businessmen, and so on.

The professor was astounded. What had caused this unexpected result? He decided to pursue the subject further. Fortunately, all the men were in Baltimore and he was able to speak to each one. "How do you account for your success?" Each replied with, "There was a teacher." The professor decided to pursue the query further. What was the magic formula that this teacher used to pull these boys out of the slums into success?

Fortunately, the teacher was still alive. The professor went to see her. He asked the old but still alert lady her secret, her magic formula. The teacher's eyes sparkled, and her lips broke into a gentle smile. "It's very simple," she said. "I loved those boys."

Where there was no chance, love found a way. Someone might say, "But what can I expect to accomplish when all the odds are against me?" A teacher might say, "But I am just one teacher, while the children have many influences." The Baltimore teacher wasn't thinking of odds. In fact, she probably wasn't even aware of sociological problems. She just loved her students!

Without a doubt the world needs love like a parched desert needs water. Everyone can make a positive contribution to the peace of the whole world by following Jesus' injunction to love one another. But more personally, love can help your relationship with your employer or employees, it can create an atmosphere conducive to swaying crowds or selling soap to individuals.

Perhaps we should take Professor Sorokin's words, *love is the only truly creative force in the world,* seriously.

## Jesus and the Passover Feast

The word *religion* comes from the Latin word that means "to bind together." Isn't it interesting that religions, which should be a uniting force, tend to be divisive? Did you know that the Lord's Supper, celebrated by Christians in Holy Week on Maundy Thursday, was actually a Passover *Seder*? Jesus was doing with His disciples what the head of every household in Jerusalem was doing with his family on that day.

The Passover commemorates the sparing of the firstborn of the Jews in Egypt as the angel of death "passed over" their homes. The story is basic to the Christian Scriptures too. Jesus did not debunk the traditions of His Jewish background. He said He wanted to "fulfill" or give new relevance to the "law" as it was written.

So as Jesus sat with His disciples in a
happy Seder, He said, in effect, "As long as
you are going to keep the Passover as good
Jews, at least do it in remembrance of the
new consciousness that we have shared together; not just celebrating the deliverance of
your ancestors, but in remembrance of your
own release from human consciousness and
your freedom to unfold the divinity within
you."

The Eucharistic symbology of Holy Communion has given rise to the doctrine of the
"vicarious atonement," where Jesus is the
sacrificial lamb whose blood is shed for all to
take away the sins of the world. This parallels
the Jewish doctrine of atonement, where re-
mission of sins is achieved through sacrifice.
Both go back into antiquity where man at-
tempted to appease the gods by animal and
even human flesh.

Jesus' new insight was that sin is simply a
frustration of potential and not an offense
against God. Thus to realize the mistake and
"pass over" it brings immediate oneness with
divine law. The only absolution for sin is at-
one-ment with God.

Every religion began with the goal of helping people discover their spiritual unity. Sacred symbols were originally windows through which to see reality. In time they became dusty and then opaque. Finally, the worshiper did not see through the window. He simply worshiped the window.

One of the Egyptian plagues at the time of that first "pass over" was that of darkness: "No man saw his brother." Thus, the passing over of the angel of death also meant an infusion of transcendental love. We need to remember that the Passover Seder and Jesus' "Supper" were arms-around-one-another experiences.

Today we need to wash the windows of the symbologies of Passover and Holy Communion, and thus to pass over the walls that separate us from oneness with God and our fellow human beings. Loss of unity is the cause of most of our personal and interpersonal problems. How great is the need for communion or "common-union" with God and with all people everywhere.

The true Passover or Communion, when dealt with transcendentally, should be an experience in sharing: vertically, in a sense of oneness with the divine flow; and horizontally, reaching out in love and relatedness to

181

our fellow creatures.

God is in constant communion with us. The rites of Holy Week are often implicit attempts to assuage God's hurt or vindictiveness. But God cannot be separated from His creation any more than your body can be separated from your mind. Let the festival of Passover and the observance of Holy Week serve to bring us all together in a great celebration of the integrity of our common roots in God and of the diversity of our unique individualizations of God. Could this be a key to peace?

## The Forward Look of Easter

It is the month of Easter! The Christian
world assembles in a manner unsurpassed the
rest of the year to hear the message of the
Resurrection. It is a simple, though puzzling,
story. Jesus had been crucified on the Cross
and buried in a tomb. Later, His followers
came to the tomb and found it empty.

In the play *Six Characters in Search of An
Author*, there is a fascinating first scene in
which six performers come to a stage man-
ager and plead, "We want to live in you."
Could it be that the Easter story and the
underlying principle of resurrection are saying to every person, "I want to live in you. I
want to raise you from death to life, from defeat to victory, from sickness to health, from
failure to success?"

Easter at its best is not a backward glance to the Cross, the tomb, and the Resurrection. It is a forward look to the quality of life it forecasts for all persons. It is not the story of God playing man, but of man, at his best, demonstrating the God-potential in all men.

George Bernard Shaw deals with the whole Easter experience in one sentence: *They crucified Him on a stick, but somehow He managed to get hold of the right end of it.* Easter says to everyone, "No matter what challenges you may be facing in your life, with the right attitude you can go through them, even grow through them, and no tomb of human despair can hold you back."

A little girl, looking out her front window, sobbed with grief as she saw her older brother dragging away the lifeless form of her dog that had been struck down on the street. A wise father stood with her for a moment, holding her close. Then he invited her to look out another window, pointing to a bush on which one spring blossom had unfolded. The youngster squealed with delight. The Father said, "You see, dear, one must be sure he looks out the right window."

While many were looking out the window of Calvary, a few were looking forward, inward.

While some gaze sadly at the sunset, the wise look toward the dawn. Symbolically, this suggests that it is wisdom to turn from appearances and know the Truth, to see through all limitation to the cosmic vision of wholeness.

Man is a forward-looking creature. His life is interspersed with eager aspirations, beckoning dreams, and shining ideals. He is forever looking forward to better things. His most despairing cry is, "I have nothing to look forward to." The Easter story suggests that it is more important to have something to look forward *from*. When we look forward from a consciousness of unity with life, oneness with God, all work, play, relationships, and religion become inner-centered. We become more concerned with what we can give to life than what life is giving to us. And the Resurrection becomes not just another miracle, but a timeless quality of life.

Christianity has lost its vitality because it has been hung up on the Cross, making it a religion in retrospect. There is a need to forgive and forget, to let go the crucifixion and the blame-fixing and self-limiting concepts about it. A far more relevant symbol might be the empty tomb, the perfect circle. The darkness and suffering must give way to the Presence and Power. The looking outward to form and tradition must be replaced by looking inward to oneness and looking forward in the confidence of growth and overcoming.

## Live Forever and Enjoy it

Walt Whitman once wrote: *I do not think seventy years is the time of man or woman, nor that years will ever stop the existence of me or anyone else.* Do you believe this? Have you ever said, "For a man of his age he does pretty well; after all, life takes its toll"? But there is no penalty or premium to living. All that is required to experience the fullness of life is to let life express, to live in the consciousness of limitless life.

You may be thinking, "But isn't it a fact that our ability does decline and our health become less stable with advancing years?" Yes, it is a fact, but it is not the Truth. It is an experience but not an inevitability. Age is not a matter of time but an experience *in* time. The effects of the years upon the physical body depend not upon the physiology but the psychology involved.

One of the great problems of our time is the "retirement syndrome." Many people are retiring at an earlier time in life. Plans for retirement begin almost from the beginning of a career. Much of this planning is built around the mental picture of physical depletion, financial need, and extreme age. It is wise to move with the flow of life into a creative experience beyond a career of work, but the important thing is, don't think of retirement with its connotation of giving up or going backward. Think advancement, the joyous step forward to a new and equally creative period of life. Beginning with a positive advancement plan, one may engage in a continuing preparation for an eventual transition into new activity of creative and useful experience.

Make a career of youthfulness through a persistent curiosity into the why of things and a relentless quest for knowledge of yourself and the world in which you live. Don't accept the belief that education is for young people. Your mind-potential will continue to expand if you provide a constant flow of challenges. When you stop learning you begin to grow old. When you stop using your mind and body fully, conserving your strength and "acting your age," you begin to grow old. Research has proven that persons up to seventy can learn Russian and shorthand just as easily as youths. The problem is not that you are too old to learn, but that you *think* you are.

Charles Fillmore, when well past ninety, said: *I fairly sizzle with zeal and enthusiasm and I spring forth with a mighty faith to do the things that ought to be done by me.* Can you honestly say this about your life? Living longer, of itself, is not the answer. As Tagore once remarked when told of scientific efforts to increase the life span: *What for? What are you living for?* More important than living long is living deeply. An old Scotsman prayed: *O Lord, keep me alive as long as I live!*

All-important is what you do with each day. Act as if today is the most important day of your life, as if you are going to live forever. This day you are young or old according to your thought, not according to what or how much has gone before. This day is your opportunity to experience the dynamic life of God. When someone asks your age, or when you are tempted to "act your age," remember, "My age is none of my business. My business is to keep in the flow of dynamic and creative life, and to celebrate myself!"

## About the Author

Eric Butterworth is minister of Unity Center of Practical Christianity in New York City, where he has served for more than 30 years. He conducts a program of public lectures, growth workshops, and retreats. His radio broadcasts are heard in four states.

Ordained in 1948, he played a vital role in the organization of the present Association of Unity Churches. He has served churches in Kansas City, Pittsburgh, and Detroit.

He is a frequent contributor to *Unity Magazine*. Besides his many popular Unity cassettes, he has published books with Unity including *In the Flow of Life* and *Spiritual Economics*.

Mr. Butterworth was born in Canada and raised in California. His mother was a Unity minister. Because he was raised with Unity beliefs, he says, "It seems natural to devote my life to the work of helping other people find the influence of Truth in their lives as I have known it in mine."

His wife Olga is an associate at the New York center.

Printed U.S.A.

40-3930-75C-6-97